Remember Jesus Christ

BOOKS BY CHARLES R. ERDMAN

Remember Jesus Christ

Your Bible and You

Commentaries on —
 Genesis
 Exodus
 Leviticus
 Numbers
 Deuteronomy
 Isaiah
 Jeremiah
 Ezekiel

Commentaries on —
 New Testament Books

Remember
Jesus ✝ Christ

by

CHARLES R. ERDMAN

PROFESSOR EMERITUS OF PRACTICAL THEOLOGY
PRINCETON THEOLOGICAL SEMINARY

Wm. B. Eerdmans Publishing Co.
Grand Rapids, Michigan

Printed in the United States of America

Contents

*"Remember Jesus Christ,
risen from the dead."*

—2 Timothy 2:8 (A.S.V.)

Chapter One

Events Which Lent Recalls

Is NOT THIS the aim of Lent, is not this, indeed, the purpose of the Christian Year, namely, to prompt His followers to *"remember Jesus Christ"*?

Certain supreme events in the life of our Lord have been selected, and assigned to definite days of the calendar, in order that the recurrence of these days may call to mind these events; for the association of ideas is the controlling law of memory. Among these days the most regarded are Christmas, which celebrates the Savior's birth; Palm Sunday, which commemorates His triumphal entrance into Jerusalem; Good Friday, the day of His crucifixion; and Easter, the day of His resurrection. To these often are added a variable list of feasts and fasts, to complete the round of a "Church Year."

The ancient Hebrews had a similar cycle of sacred seasons. The times of these "Feasts" are related to the number seven. The seventh day was the weekly Sabbath; seven weeks after Passover, which was the first annual festival, came Pentecost, the Feast of Weeks. The seventh month was the sacred month; it included the Feast of

Trumpets, the Great Day of Atonement, and the Feast of Tabernacles. The seventh year was a Sabbatical Year and after "seven sevens" came the Year of Jubilee.

Supreme among all these sacred days was the Sabbath. It was devoted to rest and worship. Two reasons were assigned for its observance: one, that God had completed, in six days, His work of creation, and "rested the seventh day"; the other, that God had delivered Israel from bondage in Egypt, and had ordained the Sabbath as a sign and seal of a covenant made between Him and His people. Thus it expressed dedication to Him as their Creator and Redeemer.

On the fourteenth day (twice seven) of the first month, the Passover celebrated the emancipation from slavery and the birth of the nation which every Sabbath also called to mind. After the passing of seven weeks, Pentecost (Greek "fiftieth" day) marked the ingathering of the first ripe grain. The Feast of Trumpets was the glad announcement of the arrival of the sacred month, the seventh. On its tenth day, the Day of Atonement, the appointed ritual indicated the provision which had been made for the forgiveness of sins and the restoration of the people to the fellowship and worship of God.

The Feast of Tabernacles brought the sacred year to its climax. It was a harvest festival and celebrated the ingathering, not only of grain, but also the products of the vines and of the fruit trees. During the seven days of this festival the people lived in "tabernacles" or booths, mere temporary structures, intended to remind the worshippers of the wilderness experiences of their forefathers, and to fill them with gratitude for the goodness of God who had cared for the sojourners in their wanderings and had brought them into the rich Land of Promise.

Between these Hebrew Feasts and the Days of the Christian Year, it is easy to trace strong resemblances, yet at no point are these systems identical. The "Lord's Day" of the Christian Church surely stems from the Hebrew Sabbath, yet it is not the same. It is observed on another day of the week and with a different design. Like the Hebrew Sabbath, it is a time set apart for rest and worship, but it is the "first day" of the week and not the "seventh"; and it does not commemorate the creation of the world, nor a political deliverance from bondage, but it celebrates the resurrection of Christ and His finished work of redemption.

So, too, Easter may be compared with the Feast of Passover. Both occur at the same time of the year. Each places an annual emphasis upon a weekly message; as the chief Feast of the year Passover celebrates the deliverance from Egypt which every Sabbath recalls; Easter is for the Christian the very "Queen of Seasons" as it commemorates the resurrection of Christ, that supreme event which also every Lord's Day brings to mind.

When, fifty days after Easter, Pentecost is observed by the Church, it is not the same as the Hebrew harvest festival; yet, in a real sense, it is a "feast of ingathering"; for on the first Christian Pentecost, the Holy Spirit brought into the company of believers three thousand souls and bound them together into one Body. Thus Pentecost is properly regarded as the Birthday of the Church. It became the custom of the early Christians to receive new converts into their fellowship on this annual festival. As these candidates were commonly dressed in white, this Day became known as White Sunday, or Whitsunday, and the season as Whitsuntide.

In further comparing the ancient Hebrew festivals with modern celebrations, the most obvious resemblance is between the Feast of Tabernacles and our American Thanksgiving Day. Both are harvest festivals, both are intended to express gratitude for the goodness of God; yet strictly speaking, Thanksgiving is a national and not a church holiday and is not included in the "Christian Year."

That feature of the church calendar which is most truly unique, and has least association with the Hebrew Feasts, is the season which is known as *Lent*. It is designed as a period of repentance, self-denial, and spiritual renewal in preparation for Easter. Strictly conceived it does not include that supreme festival, but ends on the previous day. There is no great significance in the term itself, which means simply "spring"; yet it is understood to indicate the forty weekdays preceeding Easter. As it is a season originally observed by fasting, the Sundays of this period are not included, because Sundays are "feast days."

The date of Easter, which determines the beginning of Lent, has been fixed by the Western Church as "the first Sunday following the first full moon after the spring equinox, March 21st."

Thus Easter may fall on any date from March 22 to April 25. Measuring forty weekdays earlier, brings the first day of Lent to a Wednesday, a day commonly known as "Ash Wednesday." The title is due to an ancient custom of placing a mark of ashes on the foreheads of worshippers, as ashes were regarded as symbolic of sorrow and repentance. These ashes were secured by burning the branches which had been waved on Palm Sunday of the previous year.

As Ash Wednesday was to open the season of repentance and fasting, the previous day was seized upon as a last opportunity for feasting and merriment. It was turned into a carnival which took the name of "Mardi Gras" (a French term meaning Fat Tuesday).

The most important days of Lent are its last two weeks, the fifth known as "Passion Week" and the sixth as "Holy Week." The latter is opened by Palm Sunday, which calls to mind our Lord's triumphal entrance into Jerusalem, and it continues by celebrating the events of the days of His life which followed. On Monday He drove from the Temple the godless traffickers. On Tuesday He defeated and disgraced His enemies who attempted to ensnare Him with crafty questions. Wednesday He spent in seclusion at Bethany. On Thursday the Master established His memorial Supper and bade farewell to His disciples. Friday was the dread day of crucifixion. On Saturday His body rested in the tomb. With this last day of Holy Week, Lent, strictly speaking, is ended; but no proper review of the Lenten season would be complete without reaching a climax by including the Sunday which follows and which, as "Easter," celebrates the glorious resurrection of Christ.

The observance of Lent, and the other seasons of the Church Year, is by no means universal. Many devout Christians believe that no special day for worship has divine sanction, excepting the weekly Sabbath. Nor is the observance uniform; some churches prescribe an extended and intricate round of saints' days, of fasts and feasts, to which almost every day of the calendar is in some way related; others limit their festivals almost exclusively to Christmas and Easter.

Nor is the observance obligatory. Freedom of choice should be allowed. The words of Paul must be regarded: "One man esteemeth one day above another: another esteemeth every day alike. Let every man be fully persuaded in his own mind" (Romans 14:5). Therefore, as the apostle further intimates, one who observes the demands of a most exacting Church Year should not be regarded as bound by narrow tradition, nor should one who disregards such demands be considered irreverent or lacking in faith.

Some observance of Christian anniversaries will certainly be found helpful and quite in accordance with Scripture and human needs. By these seasons the memorable events in the life of Christ are brought to mind; otherwise they might be neglected; then, too, it is inspiring to know that the same great realities are being remembered at the same time by countless Christians in all parts of the world. Thus a Christian Year may result in bringing more closely together all the members of the "Body of Christ."

There is at present a need for safeguarding all sacred seasons, even the Christian Sabbath. The "Lord's Day" is almost engulfed by a flood of special "Sundays," such as "Children's Day," "Mother's Day," "Father's Day," "Boy Scouts' Day," and "Labor Day Sunday." All have a worthy purpose but each sustains a very remote relation to the resurrection of Christ, which is the event to which the Christian Sabbath is supposed to point.

Then, too, all the days of the Christian Year are exposed to the peril of becoming commercialized. They often are valued, not for the memories of Christ, but for the possible increased sale of goods and as occasions for social festivities. The supreme test of all sacred seasons is this: How far do they help us to "remember Jesus Christ," and incline us more faithfully to follow Him?

Nor should devotion to Christ be conditioned upon any anniversary or prescribed observances. By some effort, His presence and power can be called to mind at any time or place, until it may become a habit to think of Him.

An incident is related in the life of Major D. W. Whittle, a comrade of D. L. Moody, and the honored father of Mrs. Will Moody. The devout warrior lay dying, tortured by an agonizing disease. One day, as Robert E. Speer stood at his bedside, he asked this question: "Robert, what thought recently has been of most help to you?" The reply was this: "I have been thinking what a blessed thing it would be if the mind, whenever released from any immediate demand, turned naturally to center upon Jesus Christ." "Oh, yes," replied the Major, "I have often experienced that. In these long dreary nights I lie awake and review in memory the life of our Lord. I recall His words and His works and repeat to myself His promises, and this never fails to bring me patience and relief."

Such a habit of mind may be difficult to cultivate; but a beginning can be made, not only in the gloom of midnight but in the gladness of the dawning, in hours of fierce temptation, and in all times of worship and of work. First of all, and most naturally, we may find inspiration and strength when, as at a Lenten season, we unite with our Christian friends in public services which celebrate the most memorable events in the life of our Lord.

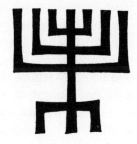

Chapter Two

Jesus Faces Jerusalem

SOME YEARS AGO a book was written with the title *The Man Nobody Knows*. The purpose of the author was to show that Christ is commonly supposed to have been a weak, harmless, helpless man, who was properly symbolized as a "Lamb," whereas He really was strong, fearless, undaunted, and correctly designated as the "Lion of the Tribe of Judah." Whoever else may have held such a false conception of our Lord, the mistake never could be traced to the evangelist Luke. In his portrait of the Ideal Man, the most prominent feature is that of courage. When Jesus is seized by His hostile fellowtownsmen at Nazareth, when the mob was about to murder Him by throwing Him down from the brow of a hill, Luke tells us how "He passing through the midst of them went his way." Or, when He was advised to leave the country as Herod was seeking to destroy Him, He defied the king with these words of bold rebuke: "Go ye, and tell that fox, Behold I cast out devils, and I do cures to day and to morrow, and the third day I shall be perfected."

The courage of Christ, however, is set forth most impressively by the very structure of this Third Gospel. In Luke some ten chapters are devoted to the record of the last journey of our Lord toward Jerusalem. Matthew devotes two chapters to this period, Mark only one, but over his unique narrative Luke places the inscription: "He steadfastly set his face to go to Jerusalem." Again and again we are told what He saw awaiting Him in that city — the scourging, the mockery, the crown of thorns, the hours of agony, the darkness of death. During all those long days of journeying, of teaching, of healing, of unselfish service, He saw clearly on the horizon the outline of a cross; yet fearlessly, with unhesitating, unfaltering steps He pressed on toward the doom that was before Him. All the heroisms of history pale into insignificance when contrasted with this incomparable courage of Christ.

As, in memory, during the days between Ash Wednesday and Palm Sunday, we review the closing scenes in the life of our Lord, we too are facing toward Jerusalem. Therefore, no more fitting messages could be found than the chapters in which Luke records those "last journeys." The material is surprising in its variety and extent; much of it can be found in no other Gospel; all of it is pertinent to the season of Lent.

For example, as the story opens, He who was about to suffer so pitifully from the cruelty and injustice of men, gives an impressive example of forbearance, of patience, and of kingly dignity. His way was to lead through the borders of Samaria; so "he sent messengers before his face: and they went, and entered into a village of the

Samaritans, to make ready for him. And they did not receive him, because his face was as though he would go to Jerusalem." This refusal of hospitality was a gratuitous insult. It was due to a mean and provincial prejudice. These Samaritans were jealous that Jesus, and the large number of His followers, planned to visit the Jewish capital and not their own city of Samaria. "When his disciples James and John saw this, they said, Lord, wilt thou that we command fire to come down from heaven, and consume them? . . . But he turned, and rebuked them. . . . And they went to another village," for there is no place among the disciples of Christ for anger, or intolerance or revenge.

"As they went in the way, a certain man said unto him, Lord, I will follow thee whithersoever thou goest." Evidently he was moved by his emotions. He felt the excitement of the crowd. He imagined it would be a glad adventure to appear in the company of the Great Prophet; but he had not considered that it might involve sacrifice and hardship. For this reason Jesus said to him, "Foxes have holes, and birds of the air have nests; but the Son of man hath not where to lay his head." Christ wishes no one to follow Him rashly. Discipleship is worth any price, but the Master wishes each volunteer to count the cost.

"He said unto another, Follow me. But he said, Lord, suffer me first to go and bury my father." He may have meant, merely, until his father was dead and buried he would be needed at home. However, our Savior regarded the reply as an insincere excuse, and He said, "Let the dead bury their dead: but go thou and preach the kingdom of God." Those who had never heard the call of

Christ might be left to the care of the spiritually dead, but the invitation to follow Christ involved the possibility of proclaiming a message of life. Surely the most tender tie must not keep one from accepting the summons of the Savior.

"Another also said, Lord, I will follow thee; but let me first go bid them farewell, which are at home at my house." Here was indecision and a desire for delay. Our Lord replies, "No man, having put his hand to the plow, and looking back, is fit for the kingdom of God." One who sees clearly the glory of a Christian life and then turns back is self-condemned. He is unfit for a place in the kingdom.

During these last short weeks of His life, our Lord realized that He could reach with His glad message only a small fraction of those in His land. He was eager to have His gospel more widely proclaimed. Therefore He "appointed other seventy also, and sent them . . . into every city and place, whither he himself would come." He exhorted them to pray "the Lord of the harvest that he would send forth laborers into his harvest." All who truly remember Christ should share His desire for a wider and more speedy preaching of the gospel, and in word and deed express their eagerness for a greater number of workers. When the Seventy returned, rejoicing in the results of their labors, the Lord saw in their success a prophecy of the final defeat of all the powers of darkness. He bade His messengers to rejoice not only in their success but in the fact that they were His servants and certain to share in His triumph.

A lawyer, who knew that God requires one to love his neighbor as he loves himself, sought to justify his lack of such love by some false view of what it is to be a neighbor. Our Lord convicted him by the parable of the Good Samaritan. When the priest and the Levite neglected a poor suffering man whom the robbers had wounded, a despised Samaritan cared for him and gave him most generous relief. Jesus showed that a neighbor is not merely a man who needs your help, but also one who helps your need.

One of His last journeys brought Jesus to Bethany, where He was received as a guest in the home of Mary and Martha. Both sisters sought with equal devotion to honor the Master. Mary sat reverently listening to His teaching, but Martha became nervous and irritable in preparing for Him a needlessly elaborate meal. Jesus gave His word of loving counsel: "Martha, Martha, thou art careful and troubled about many things: but one thing is needful: and Mary hath chosen that good part, which shall not be taken away from her." So He teaches all His disciples, that quietly seeking to learn of Him may be more pleasing to their Lord than a wearisome round of devoted activities.

During these last days of His ministry the Master gave His disciples frequent lessons in the school of prayer. He taught them by His own example; He taught them by a form which is commonly known as the "Lord's Prayer," and by such precepts as "Ask, and it will be given you; seek, and ye shall find; knock, and it shall be opened unto you"; He also taught them by memorable parables. Among the latter may be mentioned the story of the

[21]

friend who was given bread at midnight because of his importunity; thus the followers of Christ are encouraged to perseverance in prayer.

Then there is the unrighteous judge, who, to escape the annoyance of an injured widow's repeated pleas, grants her the justice she deserves; how much more will a loving and merciful Father give heed to the cries of His own children. Humility and penitence are conditions of prevailing prayer. Thus the self-righteous Pharisee, who proudly thanked God that he was "not as other men are," is contrasted with the Publican who cried, "God, be merciful to me a sinner," and who "went down to his house justified rather than the other."

The most familiar and appealing of all the parables of our Lord is that of the Prodigal Son. No parable could be more relevant to the Lenten season, which is designed to secure repentance and spiritual renewal. Many who in self-will have been living far away from happiness and home, disillusioned, disgraced and in distress, have been turned by this short story to find a loving pardon and a royal welcome in the Father's home. Much, too, can be learned from the elder brother in the parable. He has never left the house, but really has been living far away, feeling for his father neither sympathy nor love. Will he repent; will he give heed to the father's pathetic plea; will he accept the riches and the fellowship and the joy which his father is eager to give?

By His parables the Master is giving instruction not only in prayer and penitence, but also in the use of worldly possessions. The Prodigal shows how wealth may be squandered; the Dishonest Steward how it may be unjustly employed; the Rich Man and Lazarus how it may be retained selfishly and cruelly.

Some days earlier Christ had given a warning against covetousness. It was enforced by the parable of the Rich Fool. The man in the parable was rather embarrassed by his increasing wealth, and he felt quite secure for the future. "I will pull down my barns, and build greater. . . . And I will say to my soul, Soul, thou hast much goods laid up for many years; take thine ease, eat, drink, and be merry. But God said unto him, Thou fool, this night thy soul shall be required of thee: then whose shall those things be, which thou hast provided? So is he that layeth up treasure for himself, and is not rich toward God."

On the other hand, the Master would have His followers free from anxiety. He drew His lessons from the beautiful book of nature. If God cares for the birds and clothes the flowers in their loveliness, will He not supply the wants of His children? Therefore they should not be anxious about food and clothing, for the Father knows their need of these things. They are to seek His kingdom and His righteousness, humbly trusting that these necessary things will be added unto them.

There must be no carelessness as to that kingdom, either in its present form or in its future glory. The invitation to a Christian life was compared, in a parable, with the summons to a Great Supper. Those who declined to come gave flimsy excuses which showed their absorption in selfish interests and a complete disregard of the one who had offered to be their host. So to refuse the call of Christ is to indicate a blind indifference to what He has to offer and a failure to appreciate the joy of fellowship with Him.

In the case of the Rich Young Ruler, there was one who did realize the fullness of life which our Lord was able to bestow; but he was not willing to sacrifice his riches in order to secure what he needed and really craved. His was a fateful and deliberate choice; his was the "Great Refusal." Christ does not always demand the sacrifice of wealth, but He does teach us that nothing, however precious, must be allowed to stand in the way of fellowship with Him.

As Christ passed through Jericho He rescued a man who was endangering his soul by the way in which he was increasing his wealth. Zacchaeus was a "publican," a collector of taxes. That he was notoriously evil, we do not know; but publicans secured their income largely by extortion, dishonesty and cruelty; and as Zacchaeus was "the chief among publicans" and as "he was rich," his character was not above suspicion. However, he seemed to have an impression that there was in life something better than wealth. "He sought to see Jesus," and he was surprised that Jesus called him by name. Still more was he surprised that Jesus knew his need. Most of all was he astonished to find himself accepting Christ as his Master and entering upon a new life. This was his confession: "Lord, the half of my goods I give to the poor; and if I have taken anything from any man by false accusation, I restore him fourfold." Then came to him these words of assurance: "This day is salvation come to this house. . . . For the Son of man is come to seek and to save that which was lost."

During His last journey toward Jerusalem our Lord, again and again, predicted the sufferings and death which there awaited Him; but He also foretold His resurrection; and, moreover, announced His future coming in glory. In view of that return, He gave extended exhortations to watchfulness. It was with this in view that He narrated the Parable of the Pounds, the last lesson which Luke records as delivered when Jesus drew near to Jerusalem. Its purpose, in part, was to correct a false idea that "the kingdom of God should immediately appear"; but further to show what really is meant by "watching for the Lord's return." This should not suggest mere idle dreaming but active service. "A certain nobleman went into a far country to receive for himself a kingdom and to return." To each of ten servants he gave an equal sum of money, telling them to trade with it until he should come again. When he returned he found that one had gained ten times the amount entrusted, another five, but a third had allowed the treasure to lie unused. Then those who had been diligent received proportionately large rewards, but from the unfaithful servant his treasure was taken away and he received only a severe and merited rebuke.

By this significant parable, our Lord taught His disciples that, while looking for His return, they must make wise use of every instrument and opportunity to serve Him. He has entrusted to His followers not only wealth, but time and talents which should be employed to advance His cause. The greater the faithfulness the greater will be their rewards; not to use is to lose the entrusted treasure. Those most accustomed to "remember Jesus Christ" will surely be those who are most faithful in employing His gifts, and will be most joyful in expecting His return.

Chapter Three

The Triumphal Entry

PALM SUNDAY CALLS to mind the entrance of Christ into the city of Jerusalem. It is the fourth Sunday in Lent and opens the observance of Holy Week. It owes its name to the fact that as our Lord drew near to the city He was met by throngs who waved before Him "branches of palm trees" as the emblems of triumph. The spirit of this celebration differs from that of any other day in Lent. There is joy, exultation, and the voice of praise; yet there are overtones of sadness and even deep mutterings of tragedy. The multitudes believed that the Savior had triumphed over all His enemies; but Christ saw before Him rejection, anguish, and death.

It was a *dramatic* event. Probably no scene in the life of our Lord is so vivid in color, so vibrant with emotion. The streams of Passover pilgrims, in their gay festal garments, are sketched against the spring verdure of the Mount of Olives. In the center of the pageant, with princely dignity, rode the King. He was seated upon a colt which His followers had caparisoned with their robes. Before Him moved the crowds which had come out from the city. They had thrown their garments in the pathway and also branches which they had cut from the trees. Shouts filled the air: "Hosanna to the son of David: Blessed is he that cometh in the name of the Lord; Hosanna in the highest."

How different were the thoughts of Christ! This was the first day of the week; He knew that the throngs which that day were shouting "Hosanna" would on Friday be crying "Crucify Him." He was torn with anguish, not because He saw His suffering to come, but because He saw the results of His rejection. He knew that as a consequence the city would be destroyed and its inhabitants cruelly massacred: "And when he was come near, he beheld the city, and wept over it, saying, If thou hadst known, even thou, at least in this thy day, the things which belong unto thy peace: but now they are hid from thine eyes. For the days shall come upon thee, that thine enemies shall cast a trench about thee, and compass thee round, and keep thee in on every side, and shall lay thee even with the ground, and thy children within thee; and they shall not leave in thee one stone upon another; because thou knewest not the time of thy visitation."

This "triumphal entry" was a *symbolic* event. Its features were not intended to be taken in any literal and physical sense. It was an acted parable. Christ did not propose to use the colt or the rustic garments of His disciples, or the peasants who attended Him, as the features of an oriental court which He might establish in Jerusalem. He was offering Himself in this picturesque way as a spiritual Ruler. He wished the people to submit

[28]

to Him their hearts and their lives. He hoped that in reality they would accept Him as their Savior and King.

Only faintly did the crowds interpret the meaning of the object lesson, only in the least degree did they understand their own shouts of joy or their praises and their prayers. Even the closest followers of Christ failed to realize all that their own experiences of that triumphal day were signifying. The apostle John has a very revealing confession to make: "These things understood not his disciples at the first; but when Jesus was glorified, then remembered they that these things were written of him, and that they had done these things unto him." Here is a most impressive message relative to the remorse and also the reward of memory. The remorse of memory differs from the remorse of conscience. The remorse of conscience consists in the pain of recalling the evil one has done; the remorse of memory is the sad regret we experience when we recall how little we appreciated the good which had been ours. On the day of the "triumphal entry" the disciples did not experience that deep and deathless devotion which they should have felt toward the Master who was yet to be the "King of kings, the Lord of Lords." Within a few days "they all forsook him and fled"; but afterwards they remembered what they had not remembered; afterwards they knew what they should have known; afterwards they understood what Christ had meant when He offered Himself as the King. There was some bitterness in that memory. There is always bitterness in recalling how little we appreciated our opportunities, our friends, our loved ones, until all were gone, and we think with sadness of what "might have been."

Yet for the disciples there was blessedness in their memory of this dramatic day. When Jesus was glorified then they remembered how Zechariah had prophesied:

> Tell ye the daughter of Zion,
> Behold, thy King cometh unto thee,
> Meek, and riding upon an ass,
> And upon a colt the foal of an ass.

Then they remembered that they had been the ones to accompany the King; they had been the ones to have a part in the fulfillment of this inspired prophecy: "they had done these things unto him"; and a glad and thrilling memory it must have been. So in the distant ages to come, we may remember that all the bright events of our lives were parts of a divine plan and purpose, and that the best of all our experiences were those which we enjoyed in the company of Christ and consisted in what we had done for Him.

That dramatic scene in the life of our Lord, which Palm Sunday commemorates, was a symbolic event, but also a *prophetic* event. That crowd of rustics which accompanied our Lord, that meek Prophet riding upon a colt, are but faint and indistinct shadows of the great reality of our Lord's return. They point us forward, not only to Easter and to the ascension, but to a second advent when Christ shall come to take His kingdom to Himself.

> O the joy to see thee reigning,
> Thee our own beloved Lord;
> Every tongue thy name confessing,
> Worship, honor, glory, blessing
> Brought to thee with glad accord.

Possibly the most practical message of Palm Sunday consists in what it teaches concerning the relation between faith and feeling, between emotion and resolution. First of all, one must be warned against confusing faith and feeling. The temptation is peculiarly great in times of special religious services. It is true, sometimes, that the emotions are so stirred by music and flowers, by eloquence and architecture, that one imagines he has experienced a great spiritual advance, whereas, when the excitement has subsided, there has been no abiding change. When the feelings are aroused, the question is, What is the direction of the will; what is the new resolve, what is the higher resolution? If they could have been found on Friday, those withering palms of the past Sunday, or the faded foliage of the less sturdy trees, they might have been grim witnesses of the fleeting and passing importance of mere religious emotion.

In the second place it should be noted that religious feelings may be an incentive to deeper faith and wise action. Our Savior made a deliberate attempt to arouse the feelings of the crowds. He carefully planned the triumphal entry into Jerusalem. He sent His disciples to secure the young colt; He willingly sat upon the garments spread by His followers. He accepted the plaudits of the multitude. He definitely refused to rebuke the disciples, and declared that "if these should hold their peace, the stones would immediately cry out." He hoped that this dramatic colorful scene might inspire real faith in the hearts of the people. This was His final appeal for loyalty and devotion. Let us not underestimate the value of emotion in our religious experiences. Cold, dreary, conventional services, at no time of the year will be calculated to result in newer resolution or in deeper loyalty to Christ.

In the third place, it should be noted that real, vital, sacrificial faith will awaken true emotion. If our religious experiences seem to be formal and unreal, let us yield ourselves more completely to the will of Christ, let us make some real sacrifice in His service, let us seek to bring some other soul into fellowship with Him. Let us, at all times, "remember Jesus Christ," and then His Spirit surely will

> Kindle a flame of sacred love
> In these cold hearts of ours.

Chapter Four

Cleansing the Temple

IT WAS ON THE day following His triumphal entry that Jesus expelled the traffickers from the Temple. That morning, on His way to the city, another incident had occurred which was closely related to the other two, namely, the cursing of a fig tree. All three actions were symbolic, all were acted parables, all were warnings of impending judgment.

As the Lord had approached the city, in apparent triumph, He had realized the fickleness of the crowds; He had foretold with tears His rejection and the destruction of Jerusalem.

So, too, with the fig tree; its withering away was a picture of the doom of the nation. Our Lord noticed the tree standing by the wayside and boasting a proud display of leaves. With such a profusion of foliage one might expect some fruit, but as Jesus approached the tree He found it was barren. Evidently the tree had stood in a position of particular advantage; the soil was good, the tree was sheltered from the winds, it had found abundant sunlight and moisture, and so might have had a supply of fruit corresponding to its rich leaves, even though the time for ripe figs had not come; but our Lord found "nothing but leaves." Standing beside the tree, and accompanied by His disciples, Jesus declared that henceforth no fruit should be found upon that tree. It would wither away, be cut down, be burned.

That tree was Israel. The nation had been placed in a position of peculiar advantage among the peoples of the earth. Its history, its law, its prophets, its elaborate ritual — all gave the promise of rich fruitage. When the Lord appeared, however, He found only an empty show of righteousness. The Temple services were crowded; the scribes and Pharisees were expounding the Law; the people were scrupulous in performing a burdensome round of ceremonies; there were proud claims of being the "people of God"; but when the Lord looked for holiness, for righteousness, for lives of purity and faith, He found nothing but empty profession, nothing but outward forms of religion. On the favored Fig Tree there was "nothing but leaves."

For declaring that the time of opportunity had passed, that henceforth the tree would never bear fruit, our Lord has been criticized by His enemies as though He had lost His temper and been guilty of the wanton destruction of property. Such an objection might have been just had our Lord not had in view a great message which warranted for its enforcement the use of such a barren wayside tree. The disciples at first may not have appreciated the full meaning of the miracle, but through all the ages following they have realized that here was a divine prophecy of what would be the fate of a nation which professed to be the people of God but rejected the Son of God.

Here, too, has been an abiding warning to the followers of Christ, that there ever is a peril of empty professions and of religious forms and ceremonies unaccompanied by the fruits of righteousness:

> Nothing but leaves, the Spirit grieves
> O'er years of wasted life,
> O'er sins indulged while conscience slept,
> O'er vows and promises unkept,
> And reaps from years of strife
> Nothing but leaves, nothing but leaves.

All this was true as to Israel and the miracle of the fig tree, but let it be noted that on the following day Christ gave an added and an encouraging interpretation of this incident. When Peter called the attention of the Master to the tree which had "dried up from the roots," Jesus replied: "Verily I say unto you, If ye have faith, and doubt not, ye shall not only do this which is done to the fig tree, but also if ye shall say unto this mountain, Be thou removed, and be thou cast into the sea; it shall be done. And all things, whatsoever ye shall ask in prayer, believing, ye shall receive."

As the disciples reach the city they witness another historic event which was also an acted parable of warning. In cleansing the Temple our Lord was correcting an abuse which had its origin in a public service. To attend the three annual festivals, Jewish pilgrims came from great distances and even from foreign lands. These worshippers needed animals for sacrifices, and sacred coins to pay the Temple taxes. It was for these travellers a great convenience when merchants established their booths and sold the needed articles near to the Temple gates. Yet as time went on, these traffickers ventured within and plied their trade in the sacred courts.

It is not to be imagined that the tradesmen entered the central shrine and invaded the "Holy Place" or the "Holy of Holies." The Temple must be regarded as a group of buildings. The inner sanctuary was approached by a series of open courts and covered porticos. Even these were regarded as so sacred that a Gentile could enter them only on pain of death. It was these outer spaces, which also were regarded as reserved for the worship of God, probably the very Court of the Gentiles, which our Lord found desecrated by the presence of animals and pigeons and by the tables of money changers. His serious rebuke condemned not only the traffic itself, but the very character of the transactions. The priests could pronounce upon the acceptable character of all sacrifices, and they were also interested in the profits from the sales. The practice gave every opportunity for fraud and extortion. All this is implied in the words of the Master: "Is it not written, My house shall be called a house of prayer for all the nations? but ye have made it a den of thieves."

A place where oxen and sheep were being stalled or sold was surely not a "house of prayer"; it certainly had been diverted from its divine purpose. It was being used not for the worship of God, but for the defrauding of men. Nor was it a house "for all nations"; only in one court could Gentiles pray, and this very court was the one utilized for the unseemly intrusion of animals and the disturbances caused by their exhibition and sale. Nor was the interference with worship the only charge. The exhorbitant prices, the fraud and extortion were notorious; and the full meaning of our Savior's words would be understood by all who heard them: "Ye have made it a den of thieves."

In expelling these unholy traffickers our Lord has been accused of anger and violence. His action certainly was characterized by decision and indignation: "He cast out all them that sold and bought in the temple, and overthrew the tables of the moneychangers, and the seats of them that sold doves; and would not suffer that any man should carry any vessel through the temple."

Surely this was not an act of gentleness or weakness; but it was not the use of force. Our Savior stood alone. His power was that of conscious right when facing conscious wrong. No violence or force was needed. As the poet declares,

> My strength is as the strength of ten,
> Because my heart is pure.

Or as another writer is quoted as saying: "If in my heart I know that I am right, though ten thousand should come against me I should go on. If in my heart I know I am wrong, though a beggar came to me dressed in filthy rags, I shall not prevail."

Undoubtedly the traffickers withdrew. They were terrified by this uncompromising, irresistible representative of divine justice. Once before there had been a similar incident. According to the Gospel of John, it was with such a cleansing of the Temple that our Lord began His public ministry. If this is true, the return of the merchants is an illustration of a trait of human conduct. For one to turn from an evil course in fear, and not from conviction, is to produce a mere temporary reform. The wrong practice will again be resumed. What the nation needed was the cleansing of its heart, and a spiritual rebirth. This is the real meaning of the conduct of our Lord. Cleansing the Temple was a symbolic act. Not merely a building, or a sacred court, needed to be purified, but the life of a nation. The Temple was the most sacred place in the Holy City of a Holy Land. If this could be desecrated without rebuke, what did this indicate as to the state of the people? What a picture this gave of wickedness, of impiety, of apostasy! No wonder that our Savior showed His indignation; no wonder that He gave an object lesson of coming judgment. One may well recall the words of the prophet: "The Lord whom ye seek, shall suddenly come to his temple . . . and who will abide the day of his coming? And who shall stand when he appeareth? for he is like a refiner's fire."

As the traders retire in disgrace, their places are filled by a very different group: "The blind and the lame came to him in the temple; and he healed them"; for He who could rebuke and punish could also pardon and restore.

Sweet music is heard as the tumult and commotion subside. It is the voices of children chanting the praises they had heard sung on the previous day: "Hosanna to the son of David." The chief priests and scribes were indignant, and turned in protest to Jesus: "Hearest thou what these say?" "And Jesus said unto them, Yea; have ye never read,

Out of the mouth of babes and sucklings
thou hast perfected praise"? (Psalm 8:2).

Our Savior was quoting a Psalm which predicted His
world-wide rule. His name was yet to be "excellent in all
the earth." The voices of the children were but an antici-
pation of that future chorus of universal praise. The
memory turns to the words of the prophet, who saw in
inspired vision a nation purified and a Temple restored
to its place of supreme glory and reverent worship:

And it shall come to pass in the last days
that the mountain of the Lord's house
shall be established in the top of the mountains,
and shall be exalted above the hills;
and all nations shall flow unto it . . .
and they shall beat their swords into plowshares,
and their spears into pruninghooks:
nation shall not lift up sword against nation,
neither shall they learn war any more (Isaiah 2:2,4).

Chapter Five

Defeating His Foes

THE MEMORIES WHICH are related to the third day of Holy Week concern, in large measure, the bitter controversy between Christ and His enemies. Let us keep the exact situation in mind. The chief priests and the rulers had determined to take the life of our Lord. There were two obstacles which they must overcome: first, they must change the attitude of the people; secondly, they must secure some semblance of fault before they could deliver Him over to the Roman authorities to be put to death.

The city was crowded with pilgrims, and·all the throngs regarded Jesus as their great Prophet. They had even hailed Him as their King. Any act of hostility toward Him might result in a dangerous outbreak; this popular idol must first be discredited.

They find Jesus in the Temple surrounded by a crowd of eager listeners, and they open the attack with this crafty question: "By what authority doest thou these things? and who gave thee this authority?" That was to say: "What right have you to be hailed as the Messiah, or to take control of the Temple or to be here as a public teacher?" The rulers feel they have put Christ into a dilemma. If He claimed to speak by divine authority, as sustaining a peculiar relation to God, He might be accused of blasphemy. If He claimed some delegated human authority He would appear to be renouncing and repudiating the very rulers who were supposed to have the right of appointing public teachers.

His reply was immediate, and so shrewd as to put His enemies into a counter-dilemma: "I also will ask you one thing, which if ye tell me, I in like wise will tell you by what authority I do these things. The baptism of John, whence was it? from heaven, or of men?" And they argued with one another, "If we shall say, From heaven; he will say unto us, Why did ye not then believe him? But if we shall say, Of men; we fear the people; for all hold John as a prophet." So they answered Jesus, "We cannot tell," and He said to them, "Neither tell I you by what authority I do these things."

He thus silenced the enemy; He had defeated them with their own weapon. Yet more, He had discredited them as teachers, and this in the presence of the very crowds they were seeking to turn away from Christ. They, the boasted religious authorities, were compelled to admit in public that they were not qualified to pass judgment upon a famous leader whom they had refused to accept as a prophet. They were thus abdicating their place of authority. Yet, they were not only defeated, and discredited, they were disgraced. They were compelled to say what they knew, and the crowd knew, and they knew

[41]

the crowd knew, was untrue. They said, "We do not know"; they claimed to have no opinion. The fact was that they were afraid to confess what they really believed. They attempted to escape from their dilemma by a lie; but there was no escape. They stood before the crowd of listeners self-convicted of malice, of cowardice, and deceit.

Yet Christ had answered them. He had not simply silenced them by a puzzling question, but by comparing Himself with John He was really claiming the same divine authority as that which had commissioned the prophet. John had been His forerunner. Those who had refused the call of John were now refusing the claims of the King. What they needed was not more proof of authority but more submission to the will of God. Those who had heeded the call of John to repent would be ready to accept the offer of Christ to save.

As His enemies were about to turn away in silence and in shame, our Lord pronounced upon them a series of devastating parables. These were short stories which told of judgment upon these rulers and their guilty nation. No names were mentioned. The hearers were allowed to make their own applications. And Christ gave them no excuse for seizing Him or for forbidding Him to teach.

According to the first parable, "A certain man had two sons; and he came to the first, and said, Son, go work to day in my vineyard. He answered and said, I will not: but afterward he repented, and went. And he came to the second, and said likewise. And he answered and said, I go, sir: and went not. Whether of them twain did the will of his father?"

How clearly such a story illustrated the reception given to the message of John and to that of Jesus! Notorious sinners who had long refused to do the will of God repented and began to serve Him, while self-righteous teachers of the law refused the call and did not repent and believe.

The second parable was the longer Parable of the Vineyard. A householder planted and nurtured a choice vineyard and "let it out to husbandmen." "When the time of the fruit drew near, he sent his servants to the husbandmen, that they might receive the fruits of it," but the servants were abused and killed. The same treatment was afforded to others. Then the householder sent his own son, "and they caught him, and cast him out of the vineyard, and slew him." "When the lord therefore of the vineyard cometh, what will he do unto those husbandmen? They say to him, He will miserably destroy those wicked men, and will let out his vineyard unto other husbandmen, which shall render him the fruits in their seasons."

How obvious was the teaching of such a short story! The vineyard was Israel; the tenants, the Jewish rulers; the servants, who were abused and killed, were the prophets of God; the son was our Savior. He was to be killed; but the day would come when Jerusalem would be destroyed, and when "the kingdom of God" would be taken away from Israel "and given to a nation bringin' forth the fruits thereof."

There was a third parable, quite as serious in its implications. This was the story of the marriage feast. It pictured the joy and gladness offered to those who would accept Christ and the misery of those who would reject Him. In the parable those invited to the feast refused to come; others who were bidden made light of the invitation, and even abused and killed the servants of the king.

So the king "sent forth his armies, and destroyed those murderers, and burned up their city." Then the king's servants "went out into the highways, and gathered together all as many as they found, both bad and good: and the wedding was furnished with guests."

Thus when Israel refuses to accept the invitation of the great King, the despised Gentiles will be called and the wedding hall will be supplied with guests.

A serious and important paragraph is added. Those first invited showed their unworthiness by their refusal to accept. Yet those who were less worthy, when brought in, all needed to wear wedding garments. All who would enjoy fellowship with Christ, and the joys of His kingdom, need to be clothed in righteousness and to exhibit lives and characters in keeping with their high and holy calling.

The enemies of Christ have been defeated and disgraced, but as they retire in chagrin they conspire to make another desperate assault and to ensnare our Lord in His teaching. They prepare three crafty questions in answer to which He will be sure to be discredited by the people or to appear disloyal to Rome.

First was the question regarding tribute: "Is it lawful to give tribute unto Caesar, or not?" Again Christ is in a dilemma. If He says "yes," He will offend the common people who loathe paying taxes to a foreign tyrant. If

He says "no," then He is a rebel and a traitor: "hurry Him away to Pilate and the cross." He requests them to bring Him a coin. He then asks what image and inscription it bears. They reply, "Caesar's." His answer extricates Him from the dilemma and enunciates a law for all people and all time: "Render therefore unto Caesar the things which are Caesar's; and unto God the things that are God's." If one accepts the coinage of the government, and all other benefits the government confers, one surely is obligated to support the government and to pay such tribute as may be required.

To render unto Caesar the things of Caesar's, however, is not the whole of life nor the sum of all duties. One must "render unto God the things of God." This should involve no contradiction; but loyalty to no party or state can be taken as a substitute for devotion to God or obedience to His laws. Usually loyalty to God inclines one to be faithful to his duties to the state. Godliness is a firm basis for true citizenship, and no state should compel disloyalty to God, nor enact laws contrary to the laws of God.

A second question related to the resurrection. This was proposed by the Sadducees who did not believe in resurrection or immortality or angels or spirits. As Christ had previously answered the Pharisees and the Herodians, so He now defeats those who correspond to modern materialists. The endeavor again was to propose a dilemma. According to the Mosaic Law, a widow should marry the brother of her deceased husband, but then, if there is to be a resurrection, she would have more than one husband, which would be contrary to the Law. To emphasize the difficulty, the case is supposed of a woman who had married successively seven brothers. "In the resurrection whose wife shall she be?"

Christ escapes from the difficulty by a memorable rebuke: "Ye do err, not knowing the scriptures, nor the power of God." As to "the *power of God*," He can provide an existence in which there is no death, nor birth, nor marriage, but in which the relationships are even more blessed than the highest relationship of earth. Such an existence with its higher laws is consistent with the facts and laws of our present life. As to "the *Scriptures*," what do they teach regarding resurrection? Christ quotes from the very Mosaic books to which the Sadducees have referred: "I am the God of Abraham, and the God of Isaac, and the God of Jacob." Then He adds: "God is not the God of the dead, but of the living." He means to prove not only the continued existence of the dead, but also the resurrection of the dead. This is the point at issue. "Life," in the mind of our Lord, means normal life, not that of a disembodied spirit, but that of an immortal soul clothed with a deathless body. "The living" of whom Christ speaks are therefore the "risen."

Our confident expectation of such a future state is based on our relation to God. If He truly is "our God" and we are His people, the triumph of death is not real and permanent, but temporary and it will be terminated by the glory of a resurrection from the dead. Many beliefs which men ridicule, because they seem to contradict the laws of nature, will be vindicated, some day, by the discovery of higher laws. It is for us to ask what has been "written," and then to believe in the "power of God" to perform that which has been promised.

The answer given by our Lord to a third question is so familiar and so perfect that one may ask why it seemed so difficult: "Which is the great commandment in the law?" It should be remembered that in His day the question was bitterly debated by the wisest of the religious teachers. Whatever answer Christ might give would divide His hearers and discredit Him as a divinely appointed teacher. His reply was surprising. He simply quoted two passages from the Law: "Hear, O Israel: the Lord our God is one Lord: and thou shalt love the Lord thy God with all thine heart, and with all thy soul, and with all thy mind" (Deuteronomy 6:4,5) : "Thou shalt love thy neighbor as thyself" (Leviticus 19:18). So Christ declares that love is the sum of moral obligation and the essence of divine law. It is significant that Mark adds the statement, "No man after that durst ask him any question."

Christ, however, had a question which completely silenced His enemies. It is the supreme question in philosophy and religion. Where is Christ to be placed in relation to God and man? Is He to be regarded as man or God, or at once God and man; or as Jesus voiced the question: How could the coming Messiah be spoken of as the Son of David, and also as David's Lord? (Psalm 110:1). There can be but one answer: Christ is both human and divine. He is the Son of David and also the Son of God. His incarnation is the only solution of our most serious difficulties in the sphere of religious belief.

Christ has defeated and silenced His foes. Now, before leaving the Temple, He warns the people against these "scribes and Pharisees," and pronounces upon them a series of solemn "woes." It may be noticed that the most severe denunciations of our Lord are directed not against notorious sinners, but against men of respectable standing who were loud in their profession of religion. This does not mean that open vice and flagrant sin are better than proud and selfish morality; but it does mean that wicked and evil conduct is particularly repulsive when practiced under the mask of ostentatious religious rites and ceremonies.

Christ does not repudiate these teachers whom He denounces. He distinguishes between the men and their office. In so far as they expounded the Law of Moses, their instructions were to be received, but the example of their lives was not to be followed. These were men, He declared, who found it easier to preach than to practice.

Our Lord also denounces the pride and vanity of the Pharisees. .They sought for public recognition and praise. His followers, however, should be humble and willing to accept the part of servants. Lowliness would be the path to exaltation.

In pronouncing seven "woes" upon the Pharisees Christ's words are the most severe of all His recorded utterances. There is no loss of self-control, no expression of malice, only burning indignation against hypocrisy and deep sorrow for sin. These words embody an abiding warning against all unreality in religion, against all bigotry and insincerity and pretense.

(1) The first woe rebuked the leaders who claimed to be religious and yet made other people irreligious. The Pharisees, by rejecting John and refusing to accept Jesus,

actually kept men from repentance and from entering the kingdom of heaven. There are those today whose "religion" is so cold and cruel and formal, or so obviously a cloak for evil, that they keep others from Christ and His Church.

(2) The second woe rebukes the fanatical spirit which masquerades as religious zeal. One may seek for proselytes, only to strengthen his own party, while he infects converts with his own spirit of bigotry and pride.

(3) There are those who believe that an oath is binding only when it is phrased in some particular words, and that the laws of God may be broken with impunity under certain mere accidents of time and place.

(4) There are those who are to be condemned for the loss of spiritual perspective. They are most scrupulous in obeying minute and insignificant rules of formal religion, while at the same time they defy the most obvious laws of morality.

(5) There is the hypocrisy which is content with cleaning the "outside of the cup and of the platter," which is satisfied with ceremonial forms and repetition, while the heart is full of impurity and sin.

(6) There are those whose influence is made more dangerous by the fact that they conceal their real impurity with a show of holiness and the forms of religion.

(7) Those rulers whom Christ was rebuking prided themselves upon being better than their fathers who had killed the prophets of old, whereas they were themselves planning to put to death the Greatest of all prophets. It is easy for one to regard himself superior to others merely because his faults are committed under different circum-

stances and at other times. The enmity of these rulers to
Christ showed that they were of the same moral character
as those ancient murderers whose crimes they pretended
to lament.

Christ concludes these woes by a solemn prediction of
judgment upon those rulers who were about to show by
their heartless treatment of Christ's followers that they
were the true sons of those who had killed the prophets
of God.

Then follows the famous lament of Christ over the city
He loved, the destruction of which He so clearly foresaw:
"O Jerusalem, Jerusalem . . . how often would I have
gathered thy children together . . . and ye would not!
Behold, your house is left unto you desolate." Yet He
adds a last note of hope: "Ye shall not see me henceforth,
till ye shall say, Blessed is he that cometh in the name of
the Lord." The time of repentance would come. A restored and renewed people would welcome their returning
Lord. The hope of Israel and of the world centers in the
coming of the King.

Chapter Six

Predictions of His Return

URING THOSE LAST days of His ministry, Jesus often spoke of His departure. He was to go by the mysterious pathway of death and resurrection; but He was to come back again. He was like a nobleman who "went into a far country to receive for himself a kingdom and to return." So after a long time the risen and ascended Lord would reappear, and in power and great glory. It is with these predictions in mind that we should close the celebration of the third day of Holy Week.

When He had defeated His enemies, our Lord left the Temple with His disciples; He crossed the brook Kedron, and rested on the slope of the Mount of Olives. He could look westward, as the sun declined over the sacred city, the destruction of which He had predicted. Then "the disciples came unto him privately, saying, Tell us, when shall these things be? and what shall be the sign of thy coming, and of the end of the world [age]?"

In reply to this question our Lord delivered His most memorable message concerning His return. The outline is clear; its surprising theme is impressively stated; but many of the phrases are difficult to interpret, and this for a number of reasons.

First of all, it is evident that we have recorded here only a portion of the discourse. Even when we add the details found in the Gospels of Mark and of Luke, it appears that here is only a fraction of the prophecy. A fuller report might be more easily understood.

Then, too, our Lord is using symbolic language, and Oriental imagery must be interpreted with caution and reserve. The facts in mind are more important than the figures, and they must not be confused.

In the third place, it must be noted that Christ is predicting, not one event, but two. He is prophesying the destruction of Jerusalem by the armies of Rome, under Titus; but He is using the colors of that tragic event to paint the picture of His own return in glory. These two scenes are so blended on the horizon that it is difficult to determine whether certain statements refer to the nearer or the more remote event.

Consequently, while there should be no doubt as to the reality of the personal glorious return of Christ, much diversity of views, regarding details and circumstances, must be allowed.

As to the present age, from the ascension of Christ until His return, the prophecy is dark with heavy shadows; yet not darker than the pages of history by which it has been fulfilled. There would arise false Messiahs offering deliverance and salvation to men; there would be unrest among the nations and physical disasters: "Nation shall rise against nation, and kingdom against kingdom: and there shall be famines, and pestilences, and earthquakes, in divers places." The followers of Christ would be hated among all nations; many would prove false and treacherous; but those who continued faithful would be saved.

However, no matter what conditions might prevail in the world, or in the Church, the duty and the mission of Christians would continue unchanged and imperative, namely, the evangelization of the world: "This gospel of the kingdom shall be preached in all the world for a witness unto all the nations; and then shall the end come." While acute differences of opinion exist among believers in regard to the details of Christ's return, all should be united in the prosecution of their common task and should be inspired by the same "blessed hope."

As the age draws to its close, the sufferings and distress are to find their climax in a "Great Tribulation." In this prediction the reference to the fall of Jerusalem is so clear that it evidently is taken as a prototype or pre-shadowing of the more terrible tragedy which is still future. The sign that the event is at hand was to be "the abomination of desolation . . . standing in the holy place." The reference is supposed to be to the standards of the Roman armies, or, in the case of the Great Tribulation, to the "Man of Sin" or the "Anti-Christ" to whom the New Testament writers refer. So great would be the savagery and horror that, but for divine intervention, none would survive.

As men yearn for deliverance they might easily be misled by the claims of false Christs and false prophets; but the followers of Christ are not to look for a human deliverer who is to be found in the wilderness or in a secret place of the city. Their Deliverer is to appear from heaven. His coming is to be "as the lightning cometh out of the east, and shineth even unto the west." He also will execute judgment on the enemy and the oppressor, for "wheresoever the carcase is, there will the eagles be gathered together."

Immediately before the *coming of Christ* there will be signs so startling and so terrifying as to leave no doubt as to the occurrence which is to follow: "The sun shall be darkened, and the moon shall not give her light, and the stars shall fall from heaven, and the powers of the heavens shall be shaken." Then shall occur the event toward which all the ages have been moving, for which the weary world is waiting, by which the work of the Church will be crowned, namely, the personal glorious appearing of the crucified, risen, and ascended Lord: "They shall see the Son of man coming in the clouds of heaven with power and great glory. And he shall send his angels with a great sound of a trumpet, and they shall gather together his elect from the four winds, from one end of heaven to the other."

With such marvels in view our Lord urged upon His disciples a spirit of *watchfulness*. For them His coming should not be unexpected; the "signs" which He had just described would indicate to them His return as clearly as the budding of trees announces the approach of summer. Even the generation then living might witness the fall of Jerusalem, which would be a type and prediction of the more distant event. How distant, no one could foretell;

"of that day and hour knoweth no man." To the busy unbelieving world, the coming would be a startling surprise. Men would be occupied in their usual pursuits, as in the days of Noah when they "knew not until the flood came, and took them all away." Therefore to His disciples came the word: "Watch therefore: for ye know not what hour your Lord doth come." Each one should be alert, as the master of a house who anticipates the coming of a thief, or still more, as a servant who is expecting the return of his master and wishes to be found faithfully performing his duty.

Such a comparison indicates what our Lord means by "watching" for His coming — surely not idle dreaming or nervous speculation, but activity and devoted service. This lesson as to vigilance is further illustrated by a series of parables, all of which indicate what our Lord means by "watchfulness."

First, there is the Parable of the Virgins. All of them were invited to a marriage supper; all were expected to meet the bridegroom with brightly burning lamps; all were to accompany him to the banquet hall. But five of them were foolish, and five were wise. When the foolish took their lamps, they carried no oil with them; but the wise took flasks of oil with their lamps. When the bridegroom was delayed they all slumbered and slept. But at midnight there was a cry, "Behold, the bridegroom cometh; go ye out to meet him." Then all those maidens rose and trimmed their lamps. And the foolish said to the wise, "Give us of your oil; for our lamps are gone out." But the wise replied, "Not so; lest there be not enough for us and you: but go ye rather to them that sell and buy

for yourselves." And while they went to buy, the bridegroom came, and those who were ready went in with him
to the marriage feast; and the door was shut. Afterward
the other maidens came also saying, "Lord, Lord, open to
us." But He replied, "Verily I say unto you, I know you
not." "Watch therefore," our Lord concludes, "for ye
know neither the day nor the hour wherein the Son of
man cometh."

The story is easily understood. Oil is the Scriptural
symbol of the presence and the influence of the Holy
Spirit. Those who are looking for the return of the Lord
must be spiritually prepared. Their lives must be like
lights shining in a dark place. When He comes it will be
too late for the character to be changed, nor can the
necessary preparation be borrowed from the nearest
friends. One always must be ready for the coming of
Christ. That is what Christ meant by "watching"
(Matthew 25:1-13).

Another parable is the Parable of the Talents. It
teaches that watching for the return of Christ does not
mean idle carelessness nor nervous speculation, but the
faithful use of the abilities and opportunities entrusted
to us by our Lord. The story is of a certain man who,
going on a journey, called his servants and entrusted to
them his property. To one he gave five talents, to another
two, to another one. "After a long time the lord of those
servants cometh, and reckoneth with them." He found
that the one who had received the five talents had gained
five more by trading; he who had received two had
gained two more; but the one who had received only one
had buried it in the ground and returned it, claiming

that he had been afraid to use what belonged to such an exacting master. The two faithful servants received the same words of approval, but to the unfaithful servant a severe rebuke was given and his talent was taken away.

The lessons of this parable are familiar. To all of us our Lord has entrusted some gifts, or "talents," which may be employed in His service. These may be increased if rightly used; not to use them is to lose them; equal faithfulness will receive equal rewards. Those who have the least ability are most tempted to make no effort to serve the Master; but all the servants of the Lord may show such fidelity in their daily tasks, in their use of the simplest occasions for service, and in their accomplishments of any work He may assign, that when He appears they may meet Him without fear and receive His word of blessed assurance, "Well done, thou good and faithful servant . . . enter thou into the joy of thy Lord."

There is a third picture, which presents the proper preparation for the return of Christ. It is the mysterious scene of the Judgment, "when the Son of man shall come in his glory and . . . shall sit upon the throne of his glory"; when He shall separate all the nations into two divisions, the one to enter His kingdom and the other to go away into punishment. The ground of the judgment is the attitude which has been taken toward the poor and the sick and the suffering. To those who have given food to the hungry and drink to the thirsty, who have received strangers, who have clothed the naked, and visited the sick, and relieved those in prison, the thrilling words will be spoken, "Come, ye blessed of my Father, inherit the kingdom prepared for you from the foundation of the world." Our Savior then explains His words of praise, "Inasmuch as ye have done it unto the least of these my brethren, ye have done it unto me."

This parable does not teach that one who is sinful and vicious can secure a place in the kingdom of heaven merely by performing deeds of charity. Those who are watching for the return of their Lord will be most unceasing in their works of loving sympathy and relief, finding in this sorrowing, suffering world countless opportunities for manifesting a spirit of true charity, and ministering to their Master in the persons of those who are most in need.

All whose lamps are burning, all who are faithful to their trust, all who are serving such as are in need, can pray most sincerely, "Even so, come Lord Jesus, come quickly."

Chapter Seven

The Anointing at Bethany

THE FOURTH DAY OF Holy Week seems to have been spent by our Lord in retirement at Bethany. He was, however, honored by a feast in the home of Simon the leper whom Christ may have previously cured of leprosy. Possibly with more exactness as to time, the Gospel of John places the scene of this feast a few days earlier than the Gospels of Matthew and Mark place it; but both Matthew and Mark, with an apparently unconscious stroke of literary art, present a picture of *devoted love* in startling contrast to one of *foul conspiracy* and another of *base treachery*.

The foul conspiracy was that of "the chief priests and the scribes, and the elders of the people" who gathered in the palace of the high priest called Caiaphas, and took counsel together in order to arrest Jesus by stealth and secure His condemnation to death. But they said, "Not on the feast day, lest there be an uproar among the people." Little did these murderers dream that this Feast of Passover was precisely the time when their vile purpose would be accomplished, nor could the disciples of Christ ever forget that He had told them plainly that after two days the Son of man would be delivered up to be crucified. He knew that at no other time could the "Passover Lamb" be slain.

The base treachery was that of Judas Iscariot, who was about to win for himself an immortality of ignominy by betraying his Lord into the hands of His enemies. The prodigal gift which, in the house of Simon, was poured out upon the Master, and the rebuke given to Judas at that time, may have been the last goads which prodded him on to his crime. He hurries away to the chief priests and offers to give them the shameful help they need. For thirty pieces of silver, the price of a slave, he agrees to secure the arrest of Jesus at a place where the crowds will not be present. There is no possibility of offering the least defense of Judas, nor of denying that his vulgar motive was avarice; yet, on the other hand, he must not be regarded as an inhuman, demonic monster. He is an example of the depths to which any man may sink, who, while in daily fellowship with Christ, does not renounce and master his besetting sin.

The devoted love was that which was shown by Mary of Bethany. She must not ever be confused with Mary Magdalene, nor yet with the "repentant woman" in Capernaum who bathed our Savior's feet with her tears and wiped them with her hair. This Mary was the pure and sympathetic sister of Martha and Lazarus, of whom we read "now Jesus loved Martha and her sister and Lazarus." In their hospitable home Jesus often was glad to be a guest, and there at Bethany He spent much of

this last week. On this occasion, however, the Master was
being entertained by Simon the leper, who invited Him
and His friend Lazarus to a feast in his own house. While
they were seated at the table Mary entered the room
bearing in her hand a flask of perfume, of spikenard,
"very precious." In breaking the flask, she not only follows a custom of the day, which was to anoint with oil
the head of an honored guest, but she lavishly pours the
fragrant perfume upon the feet of Jesus; then, in deep
humility, she bows and wipes His feet with her hair. The
mention of Lazarus and his presence at the feast indicates
the occasion and the motive which inspires the generous
act on the part of Mary; it supremely is her gratitude to
Christ for the miracle He had wrought in restoring to
her the brother who had been dead. This motive has
been interpreted by the poet Tennyson in his familiar
lines:

> Her eyes were homes of silent prayer,
>   No other thought her mind admits,
>   But he was dead, and there he sits,
> And He who brought him back is there.
>
> Then one deep love doth supersede
>   All others, as her ardent gaze
>   Turns from her living brother's face
> To rest upon the Life indeed.
>
> All subtle thought, all curious fears,
>   Borne down by gladness so complete,
>   She bows, she bathes the Saviour's feet
> With costly spikenard and with tears.

Such an act could arouse in the dark heart of Judas
only jealous resentment, and he was heard to say: "Why

was not this ointment sold for three hundred pence, and given to the poor?" "This he said, not that he cared for the poor, but because he was a thief, and had the bag [the money-box], and used to take what was put therein."

Our Savior at once rebukes him, rewards Mary, and gives an inspiring message to all of His followers: "Why trouble ye the woman? for she hath wrought a good work upon me." He is saying that no sacrifice made for His sake is wasted, none is too great. Furthermore, the thing that is morally admirable is not always the most practical. To use such a precious gift, simply to show gratitude, may seem extravagant, wasteful, prodigal; it would appear more wise and sensible to sell such a treasure and give the proceeds to the poor. Christ insists, however, that the act of Mary was "good." There is a place in life for sentiment, and there are expressions of love which cannot be measured in silver and gold.

As to "the poor," they are always with us and never are to be neglected. Our duty to provide for them is continual. There are, however, forms of service undertaken for the sake of Christ which may have, at times, an immediate appeal. Their opportunity may be fleeting and should be accepted before it is too late: "For ye have the poor always with you; but me ye have not always." At a particular time our first duty, our supreme privilege, may be to show our devotion to Christ.

We notice also that our Lord places the highest possible valuation upon any sacrifice made for His sake. He interprets the act of Mary as preparing His body for burial. There are those who think that Mary realized all that she was doing. They hold that Mary had noticed a

shadow resting on the face of Christ. She knew He was
soon to die and felt that this shadow was caused by His
belief that His death was near; it was, therefore, to show
her sympathy for His secret distress that she poured upon
Him her treasured perfume. It is more probable, however, that Christ wished to say that Mary had done more
than she knew. Actually she had not only shown her love,
but had anticipated a mysterious need which was very
near. He realized that within two days He would be
crucified. Mary was accepting a last opportunity of showing her devotion: "In that she hath poured this ointment
on my body, she did it for my burial." So in the future
we shall learn that every sacrifice made for the sake of
Christ will be found to mean more than we had intended
or supposed.

Thus our Lord adds this surprising word: "Verily I say
to you, Wheresoever this gospel shall be preached in the
whole world, there shall also this, that this woman hath
done, be told for a memorial of her." Thus the influence
of a sacrifice made for the sake of Christ can never be
lost. When Mary had poured out the ointment on the
head and feet of our Lord, "the house was filled with the
odor of the ointment"; but more than that, the whole
world, wherever the gospel has been preached, has been
filled with the fragrance of this deed of devotion. The
memory of this sacrificial gift has inspired countless followers of Christ to pour out their lives in His service, as
in gratitude they have yielded to Him their allegiance
and their love.

Chapter Eight

Washing the Disciples' Feet

NOT EVERYONE WHO observes Holy Week knows what is meant by "Maundy Thursday," and at least some are perplexed by the word "Maundy." It is from the Latin *mandatum,* meaning "a command," and the word designates the day because on Thursday evening of this week our Lord gave to His disciples His "New Commandment" — "That ye love one another; as I have loved you, that ye also love one another." To appreciate this command more fully it may be well to review the scene at which the words were spoken. As the disciples were accompanying Christ to the Upper Room where the Passover Supper was to be served, or as they entered the room and were selecting at the table the seats of most honor, a dispute arose as to which of them should be accounted greatest.

Unhappily, it was not the first time the question had been discussed by them; and unhappily, too, the spirit of pride and jealousy and anger and selfish ambition never has been fully banished from the circles of Christian disciples. On a former occasion Christ had assured His followers that the true measure of greatness is to be found in unselfish service. These had been His words, "Ye know that they which are accounted to rule over the Gentiles exercise lordship over them; and their great ones exercise authority upon them. But so shall it not be among you: but whosoever will be great among you, shall be your minister. . . . For even the Son of man came not to be ministered unto, but to minister, and to give his life as a ransom for many."

Now on this Thursday evening He enforces His teaching by a striking object lesson which makes plain the majesty, the modes, and the motive of Christian service. "He riseth from supper, and laid aside his garments, and took a towel, and girded himself. After that he poureth water into a basin and began to wash his disciples' feet, and to wipe them with the towel wherewith he was girded." Evidently no servant had appeared to perform this necessary menial task. Each disciple had been afraid to assume the role of a slave while arguing his own superiority, but when Jesus stooped to perform this humble gracious act there could be no further dispute as to relative greatness. There was only One among them who was great. By His act all the disciples were dwarfed into insignificance. There could be no degrees of· eminence among the infinitely small. How plainly the disciples must have seen their own stupidity; any one of them might have done what they saw the Master do! They surely perceived that nothing is so mean and contemptible as arrogance and pride, nothing so noble, so royal, as humble, self-forgetful service.

Thus it was that Jesus illustrated, not only the majesty of service, but also its various modes. First of all, He wished to give His disciples physical relief. In that eastern country no guests could have been comfortable at dinner unless water first had been poured over their feet. So the disciples, who had come into the city after a walk over dusty highways, needed, as they took their places for the Passover feast, exactly the service which our Lord rendered. He had a real concern for their bodily comfort and their peace of mind.

The world today, more than in any other age, is in need of physical relief. Countless millions are hungry, cold and in prison, homeless and helpless. As never before, the followers of Christ are called upon to follow in His steps and to do all that in them lies to relieve those who are in dire distress. Even in our homes of comfort and of peace, there are countless servants of the King who are expected to devote all their lives to providing for the daily needs of others. Many names which stand highest on the honor-roll of heroes are those of men and of women who have served the world by combatting disease, by aiding the helpless, and by rescuing sufferers from the ravages of famine and pestilence and war.

There is an even higher form of service. It is in the moral and spiritual sphere. This was the purpose and this the achievement of our Lord. He stooped to wash His disciples' feet, but in so doing He cleansed their hearts. As He resumed His place at the table, the bitter dispute had been silenced, the envy and ill-will and pride had given way to sorrow and shame for their foolish boasts, to affection for each other, and to admiration for their princely Lord.

So today, for those who "remember Jesus Christ," it is possible to follow His example, and by deeds of lowly service and by words of sympathy, to restore those who have fallen below their cherished ideals, and to lift the burden of anger and jealousy and hatred from their embittered souls.

It is said that a wretched leper refused to accept a message of sympathy from Saint Francis of Assisi; but when the Saint had stooped and bathed the festering body with his own hands, then the repentant sufferer gladly received from him the needed words of comfort and of hope. Thus physical acts of lowly service can be used as instruments of moral relief and means of lifting hopeless men to higher levels of life.

There is a third form of service which, however, only Christ can render; it is that of cleansing from the guilt and stain of sin. This He alone can give. Of such service Christ is speaking in His memorable dialogue with Simon Peter. As He approaches the disciple, to do for him as He had done for the others, Peter cries out in dismay: "Lord, dost thou wash my feet?" "Jesus answered and said unto him, What I do thou knowest not now; but thou shalt know hereafter." What did Peter not know then, and afterwards come to understand? He did not then appreciate the fact that in stooping to wash His disciples' feet, Christ was giving a faint picture of His whole redeeming mission. He had laid aside His "existence form as God"; He had taken on Him "the form of a servant" and had been"made in the likeness of men"; He was to become "obedient unto death, even the death of the cross," that

He might give spiritual cleansing and new life to those who put their trust in Him.

All this Peter did not understand at the time, and so he cried out in passionate protest: "Thou shalt never wash my feet." Jesus answered him with a stern reproof, "If I wash thee not, thou hast no part with me." Surely Jesus meant much more than to say that unless washed by Him Peter could not partake of the supper which had been prepared, or even could not share the fellowship of the Lord. Christ was stating the solemn truth that, unless cleansed by Him from the guilt and power of sin, no one could be His disciple, no one could share His life, no one could have a place in His kingdom.

Peter now turns to another extreme. As he had contradicted his Lord concerning the fact, he now is mistaken as to the extent of the necessary cleansing: "Lord, not my feet only, but also my hands and my head." He is implying that he had made a mistake in his former words. He now admits the need of cleansing, but fails to understand its required limits. He would apply to the whole body that action which Christ intends for only one part. Therefore Jesus answers: "He that is washed needeth not save to wash his feet, but is clean every whit."

Christ is speaking in symbolic language. The disciples have been cleansed by their fellowship with Him and by His Spirit. They do not need to begin the experience over again; but they do need relief from their present state of heart and mind. The message may be of help to all the present followers of our Lord. Christians begin a new life when they accept Christ as a Savior and find pardon and peace in Him; there has been a total change.

They have been cleansed, "bathed"; but as they journey through more recent days their feet often become soiled; they do need daily cleansing from daily defilement. It was so with the disciples. They had "bathed" and were "clean all over," but on their way to Jerusalem and even as they sat down to partake of the Paschal feast, there had come into their hearts envy and hatred. They were called not to become followers of Christ, but as His followers to be cleansed from the stains which had been contracted during their selfish debate. They needed not to be "bathed," but only to have their feet washed.

They were already "clean"; yet Christ added, "But not all of you." For He knew that Judas was to betray Him. This was why He said, "You are not all clean." The question often is asked, Was Judas a true believer who, under the stress of temptation, fell away from Christ, or is it to be understood that he never had been a Christian? The answer of Christ seems decisive: "You are not all clean."

The pathetic fact is this. A man may be enrolled among Christian disciples; he may be in their company for years, he may even be the treasurer of a church, as Judas was, and yet he may not be a renewed soul, and may never have received the spiritual cleansing which Christ can give. On the other hand, one who had surrendered his life to Christ, and has been cleansed from sin, may find that his feet have been stained by the dust of the world's highway. He should seek the cleansing which his Lord is able and ready to supply.

In the record of this memorable incident, the feature most emphasized is the motive which impelled the Master to render this unusual service. The motive was love, un-faltering, unfailing, unforgetting love. It is with this statement the story opens, and it closes with the command that all His followers should imitate His example. These are the first arresting words: "Having loved his own which were in the world, he loved them unto the end." Probably "to the end" means "to the uttermost," or "perfectly," or "with a perfect love."

Christ showed this by His forgetfulness of self. He knew that "his hour was come that he should depart out of this world unto the Father," and He knew that He was to go by the dreadful way of the cross, and that on this very night the journey would begin. Yet His thought is not centered upon His own peril and anguish, but upon the needs of His disciples.

Christ further showed His love in that He fully realized His divine origin and destiny; He knew "that the Father had given all things into his hands, and that he was come from God, and went to God"; yet He was willing to serve His disciples as a slave, and He stooped to wash their feet.

The very character of these disciples emphasized the greatness of Christ's love for them. They did not appre-ciate Him; they did not understand Him. These peasants, now, in the very presence of the King, were showing their stupid pride and anger in a dispute as to which of them should be accounted greatest in His kingdom.

Yes, there is Judas, just ready to betray the Master, having bartered his own soul for a few pieces of silver. His feet Jesus bathed, knowing that they were about to carry the traitor to the Garden, from whence Jesus would be hastened to Pilate and the cross. As He stooped to wash the feet of Judas it was the Master's last vain appeal to Judas for repentance, His last offer of life.

The love of Christ was shown, possibly most of all, in the purpose He wished to attain. He desired to make the disciples comfortable; He aimed to remove their temper and pride; He wished to teach them a lesson in spiritual cleansing; but chiefly His desire was to give them an example and to declare a fundamental law. This is His own interpretation of the scene: "A new commandment I give unto you, That ye love one another; as I have loved you, that ye also love one another. By this shall all men know that ye are my disciples, if ye have love one to another." Thus Christ states the whole principle, the essence and the character of the Christian life. It is found in obedience to His "New Commandment." Yet it is an "old commandment," which men have had "from the beginning." Love has ever been the "fulfillment of the law." In what sense then does Christ call the Command-ment "new"? He gives it a new standard, a new example, and a new motive. The standard is: "Greater love hath no man than this that a man lay down his life for his friends." The supreme example is His own self-sacrifice: "Ye should love one another as I have loved you." The new motive is love for Him, who loved us and gave Himself for us.

Thus we can live in the spirit of "Maundy Thursday" when we obey this New Commandment and show by our lives that we are true disciples of Christ, declaring our love for one another by lowly sympathetic service.

[71]

Wherever in the world I am,
  In whatsoe'er estate,
I have a fellowship with hearts
  To keep and cultivate,
And a work of lowly love to do
  For the Lord on whom I wait.

Chapter Nine

The Last Supper

THERE IS NO TIME more fitting for observing the "Lord's Supper" than the evening of "Maundy Thursday," for we read,

> that the Lord Jesus the *same night in which he was betrayed* took bread: and when he had given thanks, he broke it, and said, Take, eat: this is my body, which is broken for you: this do in remembrance of me. After the same manner also he took the cup, when he had supped, saying, This cup is the new testament in my blood: this do ye, as oft as ye drink it, in remembrance of me.

By this simple ceremony our Lord instituted the supreme form of Christian worship.

He had spent the day in retirement at Bethany. Full well did He know that the night and the morrow were to bring Him agony, torture, and death. What His thoughts may have been, none need to inquire. Who would venture, even in imagination, to intrude upon the sacred silence of that lonely burdened soul? Only this should be noted: while there is no mention of concern for Himself, there are indications that His thoughts continually turned toward His disciples and upon the message He would bring them at the evening meal. This meal was to be a Passover Supper. He knew what it would mean to them and to Him. We recall that when He sat at the table with His disciples, He disclosed something of the burden He had been carrying for them during the day: "With desire I have desired to eat this passover with you before I suffer: for I say unto you, I will not any more eat thereof, until it be fulfilled in the kingdom of God."

Earlier in the day He had sent Peter and John into the city to make preparation for this Paschal Feast. His instructions to them had been mysterious. He told them that, as they entered the city, they would meet a stranger bearing a jar of water. They should follow him, and wherever he entered they should say to the householder, "The Master saith unto thee, where is the guest chamber, where I shall eat the passover with my disciples? And he shall show you a large upper room furnished: there make ready. And they went, and found as he had said unto them; and they made ready the passover."

This householder must have been a friend of our Lord, otherwise he could not have understood the words addressed to him. It is not certain that he had any intimation of the honor which was to be his in entertaining such a guest; but at the Passover season, as the city was crowded with pilgrims, he may have made preparation for extending hospitality even to strangers. His guest room was furnished and ready, which some readers understand to mean that couches had been placed about a table and that even some necessary provisions were ready for the supper. There must be wine for the feast, and cakes of unleavened bread, and bitter herbs. Whatever was lacking, the disciples would purchase, and above all else they must secure a lamb which was offered as a sacrifice at eventide and then prepared to furnish the main substance of the sacred meal.

When all was ready Jesus arrived and "sat down with the twelve." The usual ritual of the Paschal Supper was observed. The unleavened bread was broken. Four cups of wine were poured out, each of a half tumbler, and diluted with an equal amount of water. The lamb was eaten. Thanksgivings were offered. Then, before the supper was ended, "as they were eating, Jesus took bread, and blessed it, and brake it, and gave it to the disciples, and said, Take, eat; this is my body. And he took the cup, and gave thanks, and gave it to them, saying, Drink ye all of it; for this is my blood of the new testament, which is shed for many for the remission of sins."

Thus the most sacred of Hebrew feasts was brought into immediate connection with the most holy service of the Christian Church. In fact, it is right to conclude that the latter took the place of the former. In a real sense the Last Supper was the last Passover, and the Last Passover was the first observance of the Christian sacrament.

So closely related are these two ordinances that it is instructive to compare them. Both pointed the worshippers to the past and also to the future; both were historic, both prophetic. Passover called to mind a great national deliverance, when the angel of death passed over the homes of the Israelites, but entered the home of every Egyptian; when the heart of the cruel Pharaoh was broken and Israel was set free. Yet the celebration of this deliverance was a prophecy of a still greater salvation, when the Lamb of God was to be sacrificed and eternal life secured for all who put their trust in Him.

So, too, the Lord's Supper points back to the great deliverance wrought on Calvary, and forward to the completion of redemption and the perfecting of the kingdom when the Lord returns, for "as often as ye eat this bread, and drink this cup, ye do show the Lord's death till he comes."

The story of this Passover Feast should be of vital interest to all persons in every place who would partake worthily of the Supper of our Lord.

(1) There was a place prepared. This is the meaning of the cryptic instructions given by Jesus to Peter and John. He did not mention to them the name of His host nor the host's place of residence. With divine prevision He told them of a man they would meet bearing a jar of water, whom they were to follow into the home of His host; but with evident prudence He mentions no name or place, for Judas would have heard and would have reported the facts to the enemies of Jesus and the arrest would have precluded or interrupted the Paschal Supper. Jesus wished a place of seclusion where He could partake of the feast with His disciples and give them His last tender messages of farewell.

Thus, at the sacrament, Christ is eager to commune with His followers, and He expects them to make some preparation of heart and mind. He wishes them to furnish an "Upper Room," made ready for fellowship with Him.

This may be done by reviewing the story of His passion, by repeating a Psalm or a hymn, by reading a portion from Hebrews, or by some public, social, preparatory worship service. Whatever our practice may be, if our Lord is to speak to us at His table our hearts should be, for the hour, places of secret, sacred tryst.

(2) The unique and central feature of the Feast was the provision of the Paschal Lamb. Of this, all worshippers must partake; without this sacrifice no feast could be observed. So at the Last Supper the central Figure was that of Christ. No artist would think of painting that scene unless all the attention was centered on Him who is indeed the Lamb of God. Thus as we enter upon the observance of the Lord's Supper, it should be with a serious endeavor to fix our thoughts upon the Lord Himself. Here, as at no other time, we must *"remember Jesus Christ."* We must have in mind His explicit command: "This do in remembrance of me."

It also was necessary to provide, for this Supper, bitter herbs and unleavened bread. The former were symbols of repentance. Thus, at the Lord's table, sorrow for sin and a sense of unworthiness will be felt by true worshippers. Unleavened bread was a symbol of freedom from sin, so all who partake of the Lord's Supper should do so with a new resolution for holy living.

(3) Judas was excluded from the sacrament. At least, such seems to be the best interpretation of the story. He certainly had been present during a large portion of the Paschal Supper. He had seen our Lord stoop and wash his traitorous feet; but when this last tender appeal for repentance had failed, "Satan entered into him"; and

Jesus said to him, "That thou doest [what you are going to do], . . . do quickly." "He went immediately out; and it was night." Then followed those messages from the lips of our Lord which He addressed to the other disciples, and which are incomparable for their sympathy and cheer and hope.

Whatever may have been true of Judas, it is beyond question that, at the sacrament, all traitorous thoughts must be dismissed from the mind, if one is to receive a message from the Master. It is futile to partake of the sacred symbols if one is conscious that he is nurturing hatred toward a fellow Christian, or if he is intending to continue some evil practice or to cherish some secret sin. Unless there is something corresponding to the bitter herbs and the unleavened bread, one cannot expect to hear the words of his Lord: "Peace I leave with you, my peace I give unto you. . . . Let not your heart be troubled, neither let it be afraid."

(4) The meaning of the sacrament was clearly set forth by our Lord as He instituted the sacred ordinance. "Jesus took bread . . . and brake it . . . and said, Take, eat: this is my body, which is broken for you. . . . He took the cup . . . saying, This cup is the new testament in my blood." He thus indicated that the broken bread and outpoured wine were symbols of His approaching death; and further, that this death, as that of the true Paschal Lamb, was to be sacrificial, atoning, redeeming, and designed to bring men into right relation to God. Further still, as bread and wine were nourishment for the body, so those united to Christ by faith would receive from Him

[78]

new spiritual strength. Then, too, as this supper was a scene of fellowship, so all who became partakers of Christ would belong to one body of believers. Consequently this supper of our Lord properly has been called the "Holy Communion."

(5) The spirit of the Passover was one of hope. It was so on that historic night, when in Egypt the Feast was first offered. The enslaved tribes of Israel were assured that their deliverance had come. They were to eat the Passover in a spirit of expectancy, with their "loins girded," with shoes on their feet, with staff in hand, ready to begin the march. They were about to be led out of their cruel bondage and to be established as the People of God, henceforth to observe this Feast as celebrating the birth of the nation.

Just so truly did Christ, in instituting His Supper, assure His followers that it would ever point them forward to a more glorious future deliverance. He was about to partake with His followers of the sacramental wine. It was to be a farewell supper, but He declared: "I say unto you, I will not drink henceforth of this fruit of the vine, until that day when I drink it new with you in my Father's kingdom." So whenever they observed the Supper, in the days to come, they were to do so with glad expectation. They were to be like the ancient Israelites, each one of whom was ready to start on the journey toward the Land of Promise when the trumpet sounded and the Deliverer issued His command.

(6) The Supper of our Lord should be a time of thanksgiving. Such was the character of the Passover

Feast. According to the Jewish ritual the ceremony began with a twofold expression of gratitude; it included hymns, such as Psalms 113 and 114, and closed with Psalms 115-118, known as the second part of the "Hallel." It was probably this expression of praise which was used by Christ and His disciples when it is recorded that "when they had sung an hymn, they went out into the mount of Olives." This note of gratitude was sounded when our Lord instituted the Sacrament: "He took the cup, and gave thanks. . . . He took bread, and gave thanks." It is from the Latin and the Greek words for "thanks" that we derive the English term "Eucharist," which is a proper designation of the sacrament. Therefore the observance, while serious, should not be sad and mournful, but characterized by gladness and joy. The words of the hymn properly may be kept in mind: "This is the hour of banquet and of song."

(7) The sacrament should summon all partakers to a humble dedication to the service of the Master. It should be humble, for we all realize that we are no stronger than the disciples. They sang the hymn and went out to the Mount where they all declared their willingness to die for their Lord, and then they all forsook Him and fled. However, they came in time to understand all that the sacred Supper had meant. They then realized that on the next day He had died for them, and they became willing to lay down their lives for Him; and upon them as a foundation the Lord built His Church. His word to them was "watch and pray." This warning should come to us in the very silence of the sacramental service as we recall

His warning. Yet conscious of our weakness and confident in the grace He can supply, we should go forward, not to failure and disgrace, but to joyous and loyal service. We should realize that "He died for all that they that live should henceforth not live unto themselves but unto him who for their sakes died and rose again."

Chapter Ten

The Master's Farewell

N O PARTING WORDS have ever been spoken which are more tender, more full of meaning than those which our Lord spoke when, with His disciples, He had observed the Passover Supper for the last time. The disciples were in need of cheer. They had been told before that their Master was to be crucified. Now, while at the table, they learned that one of them would betray Him, that Peter would deny Him, and that the time of His own suffering had come. Most distressing of all, He was about to go whither they could not follow.

The first note of comfort, therefore, is one which often has given relief to hearts torn by the pain of approaching separation, namely: there surely will be a reunion. Few words of Scripture are more familiar and more precious than these:

> Let not your heart be troubled: ye believe in God, believe also in me. In my Father's house are many mansions: if it were not so, I would have told you. I go to prepare a place for you. And if I go and prepare a place for you, I will come again, and receive

you unto myself; that where I am, there ye may
be also.

Thus, Jesus was saying to His disciples that He was
about to return to His Father's house; He was going
home. There He would prepare a welcome for them as
His guests, and some day He would return to meet them.
Their union and fellowship would then be complete.

With this assurance the followers of Christ, through all
the ages, have been comforted. Belief in God, as revealed
in Christ, has been the specific remedy for troubled
hearts. The disciples, however, were perplexed. Our Lord
was expecting to return to the Father by the way of death
and resurrection. This should have been understood.
"Whither I go ye know, and the way ye know," but they
did not understand. They thought He was to go away to
some place on earth. Not in rude contradiction, but with
a cry for light, Thomas exclaims, "Lord, we know not
whither thou goest; and how can we know the way?" The
mysterious reply of Jesus indicates that He is going to the
Father, and that in reality *He is Himself the way to the
Father*. He is declaring the marvelous truth, that, if any-
one now wishes to find God, or at last to enter the Father's
house, Christ is the Way: "I am the way, the truth, and
the life: no man cometh unto the Father, but by me."

The disciple Philip desires some visible, material ap-
pearance of the Father: "Lord, show us the Father, and it
sufficeth us"; but he is assured that the words and works
of Christ are sufficient proof that the Son is one with the
Father. "Believe me that I am in the Father, and the
Father in me: or else believe me for the very works'
sake." The disciples were not to suppose that God was to

be found only in a distant heaven. He had been with
them in the Person of the Son. "He that hath seen me,"
Christ declares, "hath seen the Father."

Now that the Son was to return to the Father's home,
His works were to be continued through His followers by
the coming of the Comforter. This Spirit of Christ, this
"Counselor," this "Advocate," this "Paraclete" was to
abide with the disciples. He is called *another* Comforter" because Christ had been their Comforter, and all
that Christ had been doing for His followers, the divine
Counselor would continue to do in and for them. There
was only one condition: love for Christ. With those who
showed such love for Him by keeping His commandments, both Father and Son would be present, in the
Person of the Holy Spirit, "God in three Persons,
blessed Trinity."

By the promise of such divine fellowship the disciples
should be comforted. Moreover, while they were to be
deprived of His physical presence, He was to leave them
a blessed legacy. This was to be a peace of heart which
passes all understanding, a peace which would be
independent of all earthly conditions:

> Peace I leave with you, my peace I give unto you:
> not as the world giveth, give I unto you.
>
> Let not your heart be troubled, neither let it be
> afraid.

Comfort lay also in the fact that the approaching separation was absolutely necessary. Only after the death and
resurrection of Christ could the manifestation of the
Holy Spirit be complete and the saving work of Christ

be accomplished. The issue of His going away was thus so glorious that instead of sorrowing the disciples should rejoice. He was about to return to the Father, in obedience to whom, and in voluntary humiliation, He had come into the world. The very prediction of His death by which they were made sad would afterwards be remembered and be a means of strengthening their faith. Now the hour had come. The Adversary was about to strike his final blow, but he would suffer defeat. The death of Christ would demonstrate His love for the Father, and would show that all He was to endure would be in obedience to the Father's will.

Our Savior had been encouraging His disciples by promising that, although He was going away, His work was to be continued through them — another source of comfort. He now illustrates this truth by His parable of the True Vine. The word "true" is used, not in contrast with "false," but to express the complete embodiment of the idea or the ideal of a vine.

The relation of a vine and its branches is the same as that of Christ and His followers.

(1) The fruit is produced by the branches; yet the life and vigor are supplied by the vine.

(2) Fruitless branches must be discarded, and even the fruitful branches need to be pruned. God does discipline His children for their spiritual growth; yet in this parable the pruning-hook is not divine providence, but the "word" which Christ had proclaimed. By obedience to His commands the disciples had been "cleansed," "pruned," prepared to produce fruit; so by the applica-

tion of His word to their lives, the followers of Christ continually are made more fruitful.

(3) The condition of fruit-bearing is to abide in Christ; that is, to be united with Him by a living faith. "He that abideth in me, and I in him, the same bringeth forth much fruit: for without me ye can do nothing."

(4) One immediate result of abiding in Christ is power in prayer: "Ye shall ask what ye will, and it shall be done unto you."

(5) The abiding in Christ is also expressed as abiding in His love, and by keeping His commandments. Indeed, all His commandments are summarized in the one word, "that ye love one another; as I have loved you."

(6) By such love and obedience, believers become "friends" of Christ, and find fellowship with Him, and fullness of joy.

(7) The very purpose of Christ in calling men to be His disciples is that they should bear abiding fruit, in life and character and in souls won as followers of the Master.

In contrast with their love for one another, and regardless of their virtues and their unselfish service, His disciples must expect to meet the enmity of the world. Their experience was to be like that of their Lord. He was the most lovable of men, yet He was the most hated by men. As He had told them: "The servant is not greater than his lord. If they have persecuted me, they will also persecute you." Indeed, the time was coming when whosoever killed them would think he was offering service to God. All this hatred and cruelty would be due to men's ignorance of the rea' nature and will of God. Yet this ignorance was not innocent. By His words and His works

Christ had so clearly revealed His Father that to reject Him was also to reject His Father; and His enemies were without excuse, or to repeat the words quoted by our Lord: "They hated me without a cause."

Nevertheless, the Comforter, the Counselor, the Spirit of truth would bear witness to Christ, would vindicate Him, and would enable the disciples to be triumphant witnesses to their Master.

The supreme ministry of the Counselor depended upon the finished, redeeming work of Christ. Only after His death and resurrection and ascension would Christ manifest His Spirit in Pentecostal power. His going away, therefore, was so necessary that He wished that the disciples would ask Him more about it. They were occupied, however, with their own sorrow at the coming separation. They did not realize the issue of His departure, or the glorious result of His going away. "Nevertheless I tell you the truth," the Master declares; "it is expedient for you [to your advantage] that I go away: for if I do not go away, the Comforter will not come unto you; but if I depart, I will send him unto you." We are not to forget that the Holy Spirit always had been in the world, accomplishing the divine purpose and dwelling with the people of God; but the manifestation of His Spirit, by the ascended Christ, was to be so unique, so marvelous that it could be called a "coming," a "gift," an "outpouring," the beginning of a new work. So today when Christians speak of the "coming of the Holy Spirit" they do not mean to indicate a change of location in space, but a special manifestation in time.

The Spirit was to use a new instrument, namely, the truth concerning a crucified, risen, ascended Christ. He would thus begin a unique ministry in relation both to the "world," and to the disciples. "When he is come he will convince [convict] the world of sin, and of righteousness, and of judgment." "Of sin," in view of unbelief, or "because they believe not in me," as the Lord declares. The rejection and cruel death of the only perfect Man was a demonstration or proof of the sin of the world. Christ is ever the Touchstone of character. To refuse His fellowship and His salvation, is to convict oneself of being opposed to goodness and holiness and purity and truth.

So, too, the Holy Spirit is to convict or "convince" the world of "righteousness"; this would be by presenting the truth concerning the resurrection and exaltation of Christ. By this resurrection Christ's claims were shown to be true, and He was proved to be the really Righteous One.

Furthermore, the Holy Spirit is to "convince" the world of the reality of judgment, "because the prince of this world is judged." Christ speaks as though His death and resurrection were already accomplished. Satan would mass all his forces at the cross, but there he would suffer his decisive defeat. His doom would be determined and his sentence pronounced. Every soul saved by the power of the cross would be a new proof of his "judgment" and of the ultimate defeat of all the enemies of Christ.

Such was the teaching of our Lord relative to the conviction which the Spirit would give as to the sin of the world, the righteousness of Christ, and the judgment of Satan.

[88]

There follows the teaching in regard to the ministry of the Holy Spirit in the life and experience of believers.

When the Spirit of truth comes, he will guide you into all the truth; for he will not speak on his own authority, but whatever he hears he will speak, and he will declare to you the things that are to come. He will glorify me, for he will take what is mine and declare it to you (John 16:13,14, R.S.V.).

Thus it is the office of the Spirit to reveal to all believers the divine riches and grace that are in Christ Jesus, and to make the truth real and vital.

Possibly the supreme message is this, "He will glorify me." Therefore a Christian desires to be "filled with the Spirit," that is, to be brought under His dominance and control. Let a Christian yield himself completely to Christ, seeking only His honor and glory, and he will be working in harmony with the very office of the Spirit, and surely he will be used as His agent and messenger and granted His gifts and power.

Now the final words of farewell are spoken. The hour has arrived. The Master is going forth to betrayal and death. Naturally He reverts to the subject of His departure, but His last message of comfort is the same in substance as that which He has already expressed. He is going away, but in the person of His Spirit He will be with the disciples as an abiding Presence. His comforting assurances are these:

(1) The manifestation of His spiritual presence will follow speedily upon His death: "A little while, and ye shall not see me: and again, a little while, and ye shall

see me," not only following the resurrection, but with
enlarged spiritual vision at Pentecost and ever after.
(2) Their anguish at the temporary separation will be
forgotten in the joy of the abiding spiritual reunion: "I
will see you again, and your heart shall rejoice, and your
joy no one taketh from you." (3) The Spirit will so
enlighten the minds of the disciples that they will not
need to ask for such explanation as they have desired.
"And in that day ye shall ask me nothing." (4) They will
pray, however, and it will be to the Father in the name of
the Son. "Whatsoever ye shall ask the Father in my name,
he will give it to you." The name of Christ signifies all
that He has been shown to be as the Son of God, the
divine Lord and Savior. (5) Finally, Jesus lays aside all
figures of speech and declares plainly His divine pre-
existence, His incarnation, His death and His resurrection: "I came forth from the Father, and am come into
the world: again, I leave the world, and go to the Father."
This, at last, the disciples seem to understand, and they
assert their faith, "By this we believe that thou camest
forth from God." Jesus replies (6) that for a time they
will be tried, and their courage will fail them, and they
will be scattered and will leave Him alone. However, (7)
He would not be alone, for His Father would be with
Him. He has overcome the world; and although they
may suffer tribulation, His followers will share His vic-
tory and His peace. In spite of all the sorrow and the
mystery, He can bid them to "be of good cheer."

Chapter Eleven

At the Cross

G OOD FRIDAY BRINGS the season of Lent to its climax,
although the observance is understood to continue
until noon of the following day. The term "Good Friday"
is variously explained, but it never seems quite fitting for
the day which calls to mind the darkest deed in the
history of the world.

It was very early in the morning that our Lord was
declared, by the chief court of the Jews, to be deserving
of death. He was then dragged before the Roman gov-
ernor, who alone had the power of pronouncing the
sentence of capital punishment. Because of the craven
cowardice of Pontius Pilate, He was given over to the
barbarous torture of scourging and then to crucifixion.

The writers of the Gospels, with marked delicacy and
reserve, spare the readers the gruesome details of the
scene, and yet they tell the story with sufficient vividness
and fidelity to touch the heart. One feature of the account
is the definite mention of the witnesses and the actors in
this tragedy which centers at the cross.

There was Simon of Cyrene, described as one "coming out of the country"; him the soldiers seized and compelled to carry the cross of Christ to the place of execution. He might be regarded as the first in that great multitude who have followed Christ, each bearing a cross. On the other hand, the role of Simon was absolutely unique. None other can share the weight of that redeeming, atoning cross, and no one is compelled to follow Christ. Burdens are laid upon us, but only in free will can one "take up his cross."

The soldiers were there — coarse, brutal agents of Rome. They were performing their assigned duty, and they even were allowed by the law to gamble for the garments of their victim; but there is no excuse for their heartless "derision"; there was no suggestion of pity as they completed their cruel task. Today, in all lands controlled by dictators, similar barbarities are being practiced upon innocent sufferers. Today more forms of fiendish and intolerable tortures are being employed than in any previous age, and on a wider scale than ever has been known. Let us remember that those soldiers are true types of the agents now serving the tyrants of the world.

A crowd was there, drawn to the scene by morbid curiosity. They were passing from cross to cross, or pausing on their way into the city, to vent their spleen upon the central and chief Sufferer. They quote the very words of the charge which had led to His condemnation by the Jewish tribunal: "Thou that destroyest the temple, and buildest it in three days, save thyself . . . come down from the cross." Little did they dream that in three days the temple of His body would be rebuilt and He would triumph over death. There are those who find no meaning in the death of Christ, and have no belief in His resurrection, to whom the words of the prophet well might be addressed: "Is it nothing to you, all ye that pass by"?

The chief priests and scribes were there. They were regarded as the "religious" leaders of the people; yet they had sinned against light, they were mad with envy and hate, and they were the ones who were chiefly responsible for this cruelty and crime. They degraded themselves by uniting with the heartless crowd in their mockery and insults. They were heard to cry: "He saved others; himself he cannot save." How true this cry! Had He saved Himself He could not have saved others; but because He did not save Himself He is able to save all who put their trust in Him.

Two "thieves" were there, robbers, suffering for their crimes, and Jesus was crucified between them. To thus associate Him with criminals in His death was the last touch of indignity and disgrace. These robbers, however, furnish one of the most instructive and pathetic incidents in the entire Gospel story. In a single paragraph the way of salvation is made perfectly plain: "repentance toward God and faith in the Lord Jesus Christ."

At first, both robbers railed upon Christ; but one repented and pleaded with Christ for mercy. That his repentance was sincere appears (1) in that he regarded his crimes not merely as offences against men, but as defiance of God: he cries to the other robber, "Dost not thou fear God?" (2) He admits that his punishment is deserved, "We indeed [are condemned] justly; for we receive the due reward of our deeds." (3) Repentance involves a change of conduct, and the penitent robber is heard rebuking his former comrade in crime.

The faith of the robber is even more remarkable. He regards Christ as a Savior, and as a coming King: "Lord, remember me when thou comest in thy kingdom." Such an expression of submission and trust is of the very essence of faith.

Another witness of the crucifixion is to be remembered, namely, the Roman centurion who was in command of the soldiers. When he saw the nature of the Savior's death with the attendant circumstance of the trembling earth and the darkened skies, "he glorified God, saying, Certainly this was a righteous man." He was a fit representative of the several centurions who appear in the pages of the New Testament. They were all men of high character, and seemed to be prophetic of that great army of Gentiles who, some day, were to be enrolled as soldiers of the cross.

The most pathetic group who were witnesses of the crucifixion was composed of those who had been closely associated with Christ. Among them was John the beloved disciple, Mary the mother of Jesus, Mary Magdalene, and others who had followed Him from Galilee. These at first approached the cross near enough to hear the words which fell from the lips of the Sufferer, but later they withdrew to a distance, with agony of heart, to watch the end.

Other words were spoken which they could not hear, but which were reported to them, and which became a priceless heritage to the Christian church. Indeed, meditations upon these Seven Words from the Cross form the essential feature in the observance of Good Friday. These messages usually are delivered at a public service conducted between twelve and three, the hours when, at the crucifixion, the skies were darkened and the anguish of Christ was supreme.

(1) Christ spoke the first of these words as a prayer for His tormentors: "Father, forgive them, for they know not what they do." His petition, however, need not be limited to the soldiers. The Sufferer, in His divine compassion, must have included the priests and the people and all who were guilty of His death. Such sympathy is a summons to all who may be rejecting Him. He is an Intercessor, ready to plead for all who may turn to Him in trust and obedience.

(2) The second word gives assurance of salvation to all who repent and believe: "To day shalt thou be with me in paradise." Salvation is not won by good works, although good works are certain to follow and to become the evidences of sincere repentance and faith. Here was a man who never had been free from crime, who in his last hour was assured that he would accompany to Paradise the Savior in whom he had put his trust. Nor does salvation depend upon sacraments. It is true, of course, that sacraments are memorials of salvation and that they ought to be observed in obedience to the Master's command; but here is a man who without observing any Christian rites is ushered into Paradise.

Nor is there any intimation of Purgatory here. Surely here was a man who, if any, needed to be purified through suffering, but the day on which he cries out for mercy is the same day on which he enters upon eternal blessedness. One is thus encouraged to believe that "the souls of believers are at their death made perfect in holiness and do immediately pass into glory."

Salvation is not universal. There were two robbers; one was saved, and therefore no person need despair; yet only one, and therefore no person should presume. The very essence of salvation and of future blessedness is fellowship with Christ: "Thou shalt be with me in paradise."

(3) The third word was a matchless example of filial piety. The one earthly care in the hour of the Savior's death was concern for His mother. As she stands beside John, at the foot of the cross, Jesus, as though unmindful of His own distress, is heard to say to His mother, as He looks toward John: "Woman, behold thy son," and to John, "Behold thy mother." Gladly did John accept the legacy of love, as we read, "and from that hour that disciple took her unto his own home."

(4) Yet, at the cross the endless intolerable moments drag by until a cry pierces the darkness: *"Eli Eli, lama sabachthani?"* (My God, my God, why hast thou forsaken me?") We hardly dare to seek an interpretation of all that these words meant. Surely they expressed a sense of absolute abandonment, of desertion, of loneliness. It seemed to the Master that the Father had hidden His face. This was the extremity of mental and spiritual agony.

(5) Then came the cry of supreme physical suffering: "I thirst." It is well known that the pangs of thirst are

the most terrible known by the human body, and this cry marks the climax of the anguish endured upon the cross. "And straightway one of them ran, and took a spunge, and filled it with vinegar, and put it on a reed, and gave him to drink." This was the second draught offered to Christ. Hours before, He had refused a stupefying drug. He was determined that He would endure the agony of the cross with a clear mind; but now His suffering was to end, and He accepts the relief offered just before He utters His last words.

(6) "It is finished." This was a cry of triumph. All His sufferings were ended. All the prophecies concerning a Savior were fulfilled. All the tasks assigned Him by the Father were completed. The work of redemption was accomplished. Of no other life could it be stated so truly as of His: "It is finished."

(7) Now the Savior breathes out as His last words the line of a Psalm: "Father, into thy hands I commend my spirit" (Psalm 31:5). This ancient hymn is an expression of fellowship. For a time communion seemed to have been broken: "Why hast thou forsaken me?" Now there is again communion, companionship, and love. This is a Psalm of faith. Surrounded by enemies David trusted in God. With hostile crowds about the cross, Christ has perfect peace as He commits Himself to the hands of His Father. This word from the Psalm is an expression of hope. The spirit is being entrusted to His Father; surely then all that is precious and dear is to be restored in a larger and more perfect life.

Nothing need detain us longer at the foot of the cross. We know the story of Joseph's tomb, and we are eager to catch a glimpse of the Easter glory. Yet as we turn away we ask ourselves, What is the real meaning of all we have seen and heard? There is no answer except we turn to the Holy Scriptures. The mystery is solved in large measure by lines as familiar as they are full of meaning:

He was wounded for our transgressions, he was bruised for our iniquities: the chastisement of our peace was upon him; and with his stripes we are healed. All we like sheep have gone astray; we have turned every one to his own way; and the Lord hath laid on him the iniquity of us all.

He bore our sins in his own body on the tree.

He hath made him to be sin for us . . . that we might be made the righteousness of God in him.

In whom we have redemption through his blood, the forgiveness of sins, according to the riches of his grace.

There is another question which thrusts itself upon each one of us: "What is for me the message of the cross?" The answer we already know:

He died for all, that they which live should not henceforth live unto themselves, but unto him which died for them, and rose again.

If any man will come after me, let him deny himself, and take up his cross, and follow me.

> Love so amazing, so divine,
> Demands my life, my soul, my all.

Chapter Twelve

The Day He Arose

A MODERN ARTIST, Eugene Burnand, has given us an interesting picture of "The disciples, Peter and John, running to the sepulchre on the resurrection morning." In their faces he has portrayed the contending emotions of anguish and relief, of sorrow and surprise, of despair and of wonder. Soon after daybreak, Mary Magdalene brought the disciples word that she and her friends had visited the tomb and found it empty. In Mr. Burnand's painting Peter and John are hastening toward the garden to learn what her message may mean. Their fixed eager gaze and their bending forms turn our thoughts toward the tomb, and instinctively we ask ourselves, What did they find, and what were the experiences of these men, and of their fellow disciples, that day on which the Lord rose from the dead?

The answer is familiar, but it may be well for us to review the main features of the story, because the experiences of those disciples may be ours, and the glad message of that day some of us may need.

First of all, when the disciples reached the tomb, the guards had gone. These soldiers had been sent by Pilate to watch the sepulchre, at the request of the Jewish rulers, who feared that the disciples might steal the body of Jesus and pretend that He had risen from the dead. While these guards were watching, suddenly they were terrified by an earthquake and by the sight of an angel descending and rolling away the stone and revealing an empty tomb. They had rushed to the city to report this marvel to the rulers, who bribed them to say: "His disciples came by night, and stole him away while we slept."

For us, too, the guards are gone. There is nothing to keep us from the empty tomb and its infallible witness to the resurrection of Christ. To be sure, there are faint echoes of the falsehood circulated by the soldiers; some men really believe that terrified disciples who had fled for their lives, boldly returned and dragged the body of Jesus from the tomb which had been sealed with a stone and guarded by armed soldiers.

Some profess to believe that Jesus did not die but that He merely swooned upon the cross; and that creeping from the tomb, He made His disciples believe that He had risen from the dead. Some maintain that His followers forged a lie for which they were willing to lay down their lives; others believe that these stolid and phlegmatic fishermen, who did not expect Christ to rise, were victims of hallucinations and dreams of resurrection. All these explanations of the empty tomb are like that of the guards. Theirs was not original, they were bribed to report it. Theirs was absurd, for if they were "asleep" how did they know who came to the tomb, and what was done? Theirs was self-incriminating, for if they were asleep on duty they surely needed the promised protection of the rulers who dreaded to know the truth. Such are all other explanations of the empty tomb; there is only one we can accept: the tomb is empty because the Lord arose. For us, the guards are gone.

The angels, too, are gone. One had been seen by the soldiers, and two by Mary and her companions, but none by Peter and John. The message of the angels to all the disciples is: "He is risen from the dead; and behold, he goeth before you into Galilee; there shall ye see him." The nature and service of angels is full of mystery. They were mentioned more than once in the life of Christ. We are assured that they are "ministering spirits, sent forth to minister for them who shall be heirs of salvation." We need not expect to see them, even on an Easter morning; but God does send other messengers who bring to us glad tidings of resurrection and of life. Some believers hear them in the burst of dawn, some in the fragrance of the flowers, some in a phrase from the Gospels, some in the fragment of a hymn. By tender hearts voices of hope and cheer are heard even in the shadow of the tomb.

The angels are gone, but in the empty sepulchre there is evidence enough to convince John that his Lord is risen indeed. There are the linen clothes lying, "and the napkin, that was about his head, not lying with the linen clothes, but wrapped together in a place by itself." This was a silent scene, not of violence or haste, but of mysterious and majestic withdrawal. These were but trifles, yet they were witnesses enough to satisfy the Beloved

Disciple; "he saw, and believed." A heart, full of love for Christ, requires but little proof to find in Him a living Lord.

It is interesting to note, however, that the evidence which brought rapturous belief to John left Peter in hopeless gloom. Both loved their Lord, but in the empty tomb Peter possibly was still mindful of his disloyalty and disgrace, while John was conscious only of a friendship on which no such shadow rested. This "apostle whom Jesus loved," was the first person to believe in the resurrection of Christ; and he it was who afterwards recorded that beatitude which fell from the lips of his living Lord, a beatitude which he was the first to know and in which we all can share, "Blessed are they that have not seen, yet have believed."

The first person to see the risen Lord was Mary of Magdala, Mary the mourner; and surely the mourner is the one who most needs the message of an Easter morning. She stood weeping by the grave of buried hopes, distressed because she could not find the body of her Lord. Suddenly, as she turned, she was amazed to see standing before her the living glorious form of the risen Christ. As she falls at His feet she hears the words which still are bringing comfort to bereft and broken hearts: "Touch me not; for I am not yet ascended to my Father: but go to my brethren, and say unto them, I ascend unto my Father, and your Father; and to my God and your God."

The risen Savior bids us look, not downward toward the grave, but upward into the glory. Then instead of the "never more" of unbelief, comes the "not yet" of faith. Are we puzzled by the dark providences of God? Then let us think of Him as the "Father" who deals with us in perfect love. Let us believe that our Lord has ascended and is now a spiritual abiding Presence, a divine Comforter, an unseen, unfailing Friend.

The man who most needed a meeting with the risen Christ was Simon Peter, who had deserted and denied his Lord. How desperate that need was, and how graciously it was to be met are intimated in the words of the angel by whom the resurrection was first announced: "Tell his disciples *and Peter*." Where our Lord found His unfaithful follower, whose heart was crushed by remorse, or what words of self-reproach were spoken, what words of forgiveness were heard, we can only conjecture; but of this we are absolutely certain: it is possible for everyone who feels the shame and disgrace of disloyalty to Christ to meet with Him alone today and to receive from Him assurance of pardon and peace.

Now, as the sun is declining, two disciples are seen walking in sadness, through the deepening twilight, toward the village of Emmaus, their home. They have heard reports of an empty tomb but not of a resurrection. Suddenly Jesus joins them and walks with them; "but their eyes were holden"; they did not recognize Him, even while He talked with them and explained the Scriptures which foretold the sufferings of the Messiah, and the glory which should follow. When they reached their destination, however, and they had sat down to break bread, "their eyes were opened and they knew him; and he vanished out of their sight."

Is not our experience somewhat the same? Do we not fail to recognize the divine Companion who is with us always, ready to cheer and instruct us, to open to us the Scriptures, and to reveal Himself to us in the "breaking of bread"? Yet there is this difference: when our journey of life is ended and we reach our Home, "we shall see him as he is," and the vision will not vanish in darkness but will brighten into the abiding glory of an eternal day.

The last scene of all is at night, in the Upper Room, in Jerusalem. It was probably the place where Christ had been accustomed to meet with His disciples. There, with darkness and danger about them, the disciples were listening to some of their number who brought the incredible news that the Lord had been seen alive, risen from the dead. Suddenly, "Jesus himself stood in the midst of them." They "were terrified and affrighted, and supposed that they had seen a spirit"; but He said, "Peace be unto you," and He showed them His hands and His side with the scars of Calvary. He reminded them of the Scriptures which predicted that the Christ should suffer and on the third day rise from the dead. He gave them their commission to give His message in all the world, saying, "As the Father hath sent me, even so send I you," and He assured them of the abiding presence and power of the Spirit. "Then were the disciples glad, when they saw the Lord."

Such, repeatedly, have been the experiences of His followers through all the passing years. As they have gathered in His name, and together have rehearsed the resurrection story, He has become to them a living Presence, He has spoken peace to their troubled hearts, He has sent them out to testify for Him, filled with His Spirit and rejoicing in His love. Thus at Eastertide they sing to His praise:

> Neither might the gates of death,
>   Nor the tomb's dark portal,
> Nor the watchers, nor the seal
>   Hold thee as a mortal;
> But today amidst the Twelve
>   Thou didst stand, bestowing
> Them thy peace, which evermore
>   Passeth human knowing.

NOTES ON THE SIGNS STANDING AT THE HEAD
OF EACH CHAPTER

Chapter One — *The Latin Cross, in early times called God's mark, is the most exalted emblem of the Christian faith, the Sign of all signs. By far the greater number of signs in the Western world are based on the shape, or part of the shape of the Cross, whether they be imperial monograms, masonic signs, family signs, chemical symbols, or trademarks.*

Chapter Two — *The seven-branched candlestick is the symbol of the Old Testament.*

Chapter Three — *The Crusaders' or Jerusalem Cross.*

Chapter Four — *This monogram of Christ is a very early Christian symbol. It consists of the Greek "X," signifying Christ and the Cross.*

Chapter Five — *Among early Christians, this, as well as many other signs of similar design, was used as a disguised Cross during the persecution of the Christians.*

Chapter Six — *These two signs were widely used in the Christian Church from very early times. They are Alpha (on the left) and Omega (on the right), after the passage in Revelation: "I am the Alpha and the Omega."*

Chapter Seven — *This is the most wide-spread and best-known monogram of Christ. According to legend it appeared in a dream to the Emperor Constantine, accompanied* by a voice saying, "In this sign shalt thou conquer." The sign is composed of the two Greek initial letters of the name Christ: "X" and "P." As a Christian symbol, it is, possibly, older than the Cross itself.

Chapter Eight — *A Cross standing upon four lines which probably symbolize the four Evangelists.*

Chapter Nine — *This sign of Faith represents the patient expectation of salvation coming from above.*

Chapter Ten — *A representation of the Trinity. The triangle is the sign of God the Father and the horizontal figure hovering above the Cross is the sign of the Holy Spirit.*

Chapter Eleven — *The Coptic Cross, with the four nails.*

Chapter Twelve — *This is a Christian modification of a sign representing the orb of the world. According to an old conception of the earth, the center of the world is Jerusalem, the place where salvation came to mankind; the lower half of the orb is Asia; the vertical line represents the Mediterranean Sea, Europe lying on the left and Africa on the right.*